THIS BOOK BELONGS TO _____

IF

TO TEACH KIDS YOU'VE GOTTA

BY

illustrated by

cover design by

YOU'RE TRYING HOW TO WRITE, HAVE THIS BOOK!

MARJORIE FRANK

judy howard

carol riley

ACKNOWLEDGMENTS

The author and publishers wish to thank the following publishers, authors and agents for permission to reprint selections in this book.

CONDE NAST PUBLICATIONS, INC. for "The Soldier," by Rencie Farwell from "Teacher's Priceless World: Where It Is Always Spring" by Kay Boyle, *GLAMOUR MAGAZINE*, March 1963. Copyright©1963 by Conde Nast Publications. Reprinted by permission of Conde Nast Publications.

HOUGHTON MIFFLIN COMPANY for excerpts from *Smashed Potatoes* by Jane G. Martel. Copyright©1974 by Jane G. Martel. Reprinted by permission of Houghton Mifflin Company.

J. B. LIPPINCOTT COMPANY for excerpts from *Cross Your Fingers, Spit in Your Hat: Superstitions and Other Beliefs*, collected by Alvin Schwartz. Copyright 1974 by Alvin Schwartz. Reprinted by permission of J. B. Lippincott Company.

DANIEL LUSK for "Children, There Are Words" from *Homemade Poems* by Daniel Lusk. Copyright©1974 by Lame Johnny Press, Associates. Reprinted by permission of Daniel Lusk.

NEW DIRECTIONS PUBLISHING CORPORATION for "This Is Just To Say" by William Carlos Williams from *Collected Earlier Poems* by William Carlos Williams. Copyright © 1938 by New Directions Publishing Corporation. Reprinted by permission of New Directions Publishing Corporaton.

Special thanks to KAREN ALMQUIST, ERIK WILKINSON, SHANA MACKENZIE and all the other young writers who have made such delightful contributions to this book.

ISBN 0-913916-62-5   Library of Congress Catalog Number 78-70901

Printed in Nashville, Tennessee

Incentive Publications, Box 120189, Nashville, Tennessee 37212

TO MY MOM: *You were in love with words, and filled my life with language delight!*

and   *TO MY HUSBAND:*   *More than anyone else I know, you believe in the power of the written word.*

TABLE OF CONTENTS

The book starts here

Do any of these sound familiar to you?

>*"My kids groan when it's time to write!"*

>*"Teaching writing is such hard work!"*

>*"There are too many other things I have to teach. I don't have time for writing."*

>*"My students are too shy or fearful to express themselves."*

>*"I always run out of ideas by October."*

>*"What do I do when a kid says, 'I can't think of anything!'?"*

>*"My kids are too young to write."*

>*"I have this kid who just WON'T!"*

>*"All those stories take forever to read and grade—I'm up all night!"*

>*"Should grammar and mechanics count?"*

>*"If I teach skills, will I stifle creativity?"*

>*"How can I ever get my students to write on their own?"*

>*"I'm not sure how to evaluate their writing!"*

They surely do to me! Some of them are my own excuses for avoiding writing lessons. Others are my own rationalizations for failures. All are the questions and fears and concerns collected by eavesdropping on teacher-friends over the past few years.

I've talked with teachers all over the United States about writing, and I've found they're interested in how to get kids to write and how to help writing grow. It doesn't matter whether their classrooms are self-contained or departmentalized or team-taught or open or traditional or primary or special ed or secondary—they all have the same questions, and they have similar needs. They're concerned about exciting ideas that turn kids on. They're just as concerned about the technical skills of writing. They want to know how to combine freedom of expression with the discipline of completing and perfecting a written piece. And they need support and encouragement for the job of mixing kids with writing.

My interaction with those of you who have shared your successes and failures with me has a lot to do with what I'm doing right now—writing a book about writing for teachers and others who work with kids.

There are two other forces behind these words: ONE is the joy that fooling around with words has added to my life, combined with the personal and academic growth that's been stimulated by pleasant early experiences with language. I was lucky to have a mother who shared with her children her love of language. She played word games, baked riddles and puns into cookies, taught us poems and Bible verses, made up tongue twisters, gave dramatic readings of ridiculous rhymes and freely shared with us her own writing.

THE OTHER is the enjoyment that has come from writing with kids in my own classrooms. Some of the most rewarding times I've had with students have involved experiences in self-expression. Those were the times that brought about the unfolding of persons and the most startling improvements in self-confidence. And those were the times that left the nicest memories!

Let me confess at the very beginning that I'm on kind of a personal PROMOTE-WRITING-IN-ALL-THE-CLASSROOMS-OF-THE-WORLD campaign, a crusade which began a few years ago and has been steadily gaining momentum, fueled by

> *. . . time spent in classrooms where NO writing was happening OR where it was proceeding with groans and pains*

and . . . frustration with highly publicized accusations that college students are seriously deficient in written communication, high school students show no mastery of basic writing skills and the writing performance in elementary schools is quickly deteriorating

and . . . my own involvement with bright college juniors and seniors who struggle to write lucid sentences or clear paragraphs.

Part of what I'd like to tell the world is the truth about how many of our students ARE writing well and about how many hundreds of teachers ARE working overtime to teach writing effectively. But I have to admit that at least some of the press regarding a crisis in written expression is true.

Not too many years ago, I used to "converse" with my friend, Ruth, who lives across the continent, through an interchange of long, detailed, intimate letters. How revealing it is today to re-read those—to look at what I was like—and to see, recorded in writing the growing, changing persons that we both were.

But now we both lead busier lives and earn bigger salaries and we've turned to the telephone for contact. And because we no longer take the time to think about ourselves and our lives as we work at translating those awarenesses and struggles into words, nor sit and ponder the written expressions of each other, we have lost a special kind of touch with one another, and we miss out on a great deal of personal growth, and we live without those valuable friend-to-friend written reflections of our perceptions of one another's development.

It's happened to all of us. We live in an increasingly ORAL society. TELEVISION, INTERCOMS, TAPE RECORDERS, MOVIE PROJECTORS, RECORD PLAYERS, TELEPHONES—give us quick ways to learn and communicate in condensed, non-written forms.

I fear today's student generation includes large numbers of

. . . kids who, as they grow from pre-school through college, are rarely asked OR allowed to fully express themselves

. . . students who don't often HAVE to sit and think about what they believe or feel and then organize it into coherent, communicable language

. . . persons who are missing the REWARDS of putting themselves and their ideas into a whole, carefully-considered written form.

And I fear we're forgetting how to think with words.

My soap-box message is that kids CAN be taught to express themselves in writing completely, effectively and enjoyably—even in the midst of a fast-moving culture that fills their lives with ditto sheets and walkie-talkies. I have seen it happening again and again: kids writing and growing and publishing. We CAN have a generation of persons whose thinking skills, mechanical writing skills and life skills are well-developed, if we as teachers are willing to take on the challenge of creating serious writing experiences in our classrooms.

Now I'm not going to tell you any nice sugary tales about how easy it is to teach kids to write OR entice you with any instant cures for your fears or for your kids' writing problems, because

. . . I believe that writing takes discipline

. . . AND, I believe that teaching writing takes hard work!

I AM going to enthusiastically share with you my strong biases that

. . . teaching writing is also fun.

. . . it's a kind of work less dreary than we've made it.

. . . it's worth the energy it takes.

. . . YOU can enjoy it and grow as much as the kids!

Since my goal for kids is to build a generation of word-lovers—

PERSONS who are sensitive to themselves and their worlds and to the power of their language

PERSONS who are willing and able to put into words their feelings, beliefs, biases, ideas, wonderings and wildest fantasies...

my goals for this book are

- *to get you excited about writing—just for yourself!*

- *to turn you on to writing with kids.*

- *to encourage you to take the risks and plunge into the work of teaching writing, and to reap the harvests of that risk and work: the closer human contact, the freer flow of expression, the advances in language skills, and the just plain fun!*

- *to give you tips for handling the whole writing process in the classroom or other writing setting.*

- *to present you with enough ideas and sources of ideas for motivating writing experiences that you will never again run out of inspiration!*

- *and, possibly, to give you a whole new look at writing—maybe even to entirely revolutionize your thinking about what it is!*

Well, now you know a little about me and what I'm doing here. BUT WHAT ABOUT YOU? WHAT BRINGS YOU TO THIS BOOK?

?????????????????

Are you looking for someone to convince you to plunge in?

Are you needing a way to combine "creative" writing with the teaching of the "technical" skills?

Did you come looking for dozens of new ideas?

Were you after help for your writers in trouble?

Do you want a whole new look at writing in the classroom?

Could you be due for a freshening of your attitudes or a reminder of your own talents in relation to teaching writing?

Were you hoping for some help in managing the whole process with your students?

Whatever your needs or motivations, I suggest that you look at the OWNER'S MANUAL right away. (It starts on the next page.) Since this book is about ALL parts of the writing process, it turned out to be six books within one. I think the owner's manual will give you a clear idea of the contents of each of those and should help you to make the best use of the book for YOUR needs.

Have you caught some of the spirit of my crusade? Maybe you'll be marching with me before long! Let's get started.

May you have as many rich writing sessions as I have had with kids, and many, many more . . .

Marge Frank

OWNER'S MANUAL

	A COMPLETE APPROACH TO UNDERSTANDING AND WORKING WITH THE WHOLE WRITING PROCESS
	. . . a philosophy and plan for handling everything from getting yourself and the kids ready—through finding and using ideas for motivating writing—to editing and evaluating and sharing
HOW TO USE IT	Read straight through, from cover to cover, concentrating on Chapters 1-7, 10 and the conclusion, in order to get a complete sense of the total process.
	AN AT-YOUR-FINGERTIPS SOURCE OF IDEAS FOR STARTING SPECIFIC WRITING ACTIVITIES
	. . . a healthy collection of "beginnings" with kid-appeal *. . . PLUS suggestions for motivating different kinds and ages of kids* *. . . PLUS ideas for combining writing with the content areas* *. . . PLUS loads of ways to get independent writing started*
HOW TO USE IT	Notice that Chapter 8 is a smorgasboard of tantalizing ideas for all kinds of kids. It includes special sections for young writers, gifted writers and reluctant writers. AND there are dozens of ideas for mixing writing with other content areas. AND—look at Chapter 2. It has more than 50 ideas for word-play and other short writing experiences. AND—you'll see that Chapter 3 has a hearty group of pages that show how to use specific kinds of motivators (such as art, music, literature, group experiences, etc.) to start writing. AND—don't overlook Chapter 10, which includes a selection of mini writing centers that you can make in minutes and the kids can use with little direction. ALSO—there is an IDEA INDEX at the end of the book to help you locate activities and writing starters that correspond to particular forms or topics.

	A RESOURCE BOOK TO DIRECT YOU TO MORE SOURCES OF IDEAS AND TEACHING AIDS
	. . . an introduction to a gold mine of help and inspiration for every teacher of writing *. . . an ample bibliography of materials that will supply ideas, describe successful teaching techniques, share the teaching and writing experiences of other teachers or stimulate kids to new avenues of expression*
HOW TO USE IT	Turn right to Chapter 9, where you'll find my favorite sources listed and carefully described. Then check Chapter 3 for some hints on using different kinds of literature to stimulate writing.

	A READY-WHEN-YOU'RE-IN-NEED MANUAL FOR SOLVING WRITING PROBLEMS
	. . . a collection of thoughts, techniques, experiences and classroom-tested advice to help you tackle a variety of those blocks that interfere with writing success or slow progress for many teachers and kids
HOW TO USE IT	The whole book focuses on some of the needs or problems faced by teachers of writing. Read the list of questions or statements used as chapter titles in the TABLE OF CONTENTS. This will direct you to a chapter you need. ALSO—pay special attention to Chapter 7 which deals specifically with the "wrinkles" in the writing-with-kids process. NOTICE—that Chapter 7 includes, at its end, a list of answers to the 14 questions teachers ask most about writing.

	A PRIVATE LESSON FOR TEACHERS ON HOW AND WHEN AND WHERE TO PROMOTE INDEPENDENT WRITING
	... *a statement about the times and methods best used for individual pursuit of writing* ... *PLUS suggestions for keeping alive the "private" writing that kids do already* ... *PLUS a plentiful supply of illustrated mini-centers to use as independent motivators* ... *PLUS a plan and design for a permanent writing center that can become a part of any classroom*
HOW TO USE IT	Concentrate on Chapter 10, the chapter dedicated to independent writing, but re-read Chapter 4 which furnishes a plan for writing that kids can follow on their own. AND—review Chapter 5 for its suggestions on getting kids to become responsible, independent editors.
	PERSONAL PROPAGANDA NOTEBOOK ON THE JOYS OF TEACHING WRITING
	... *many words of encouragement to teachers* ... *PLUS a consistent reminder of the rewards that follow and accompany writing experiences*
HOW TO USE IT	You choose any or all parts of the book to get you going and growing in your involvement with writing in and out of the classroom—but pay special attention to the introductory and concluding sections.

1

"Where do I begin?"

ROOTS

INVENTORY YOUR BIASES

WRITING . . . . and ME

1. As a writer, I am _____

2. 3 words that describe how I feel about teaching writing are:

   _____ ,   _____ ,   _____

3. 3 words to describe how I think my students feel about writing are:

   _____ ,   _____ ,   _____

4. I believe writing lessons in the classroom are: *(Circle one.)*

   very important   of value, if there's time   not very important

5. A classroom "writing experience" should involve:

   _____

6. I spend approximately _____ each week on writing.
   (Time)

7. The part of writing I'm BEST at teaching is _____

   _____

8. One GOAL I have for "Writing" in my classroom this year is:

   _____

Make a copy of this page and complete the inventory as honestly as possible. (Do it in pencil—because you may want to do it again next year or next month.)

The next page gives you some suggestions for making use of this information in your teaching of writing.

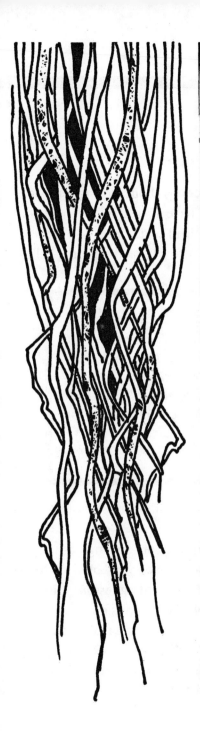

We each come to the teaching of any subject or topic with a lifetime of experiences, attitudes, feelings and talents. It isn't often that we stop to take inventory of those—or of how they affect our success and our influence on students in that area.

When I first became serious about teaching writing (especially when I started doing it IN FRONT OF OTHER TEACHERS and preaching about it in workshops), I was forced to put down on paper: WHAT I, MARGE FRANK, BELIEVE ABOUT WRITING. It was NOT easy. It WAS a broadening and revealing experience.

I've asked you to do the same, in brief form, because:

> . . . the way you feel about yourself as a writer could contribute to your bravery (or lack of it) in trying new writing experiences with your students.

> . . . the confidence you have (or don't have) in your ability to teach writing may affect the success of your lessons.

> . . . the importance you place on writing in the classroom might determine the amount of dignity and value your students accord it.

> . . . your perceptions of the students' attitudes can influence your expectations for their performances.

> . . . the goals you choose for writing will be the bases for the kinds of activities you plan.

> . . . AND . . . the STRENGTHS and TALENTS you already possess will be the forces that set directions for your students' growth.

The information you've gleaned from this self-inventory can be used as a base from which to set writing goals for the year, OR as a goal sheet for checking your accomplishments from time to time, OR as an end-of-the-year gauge of your own change and growth.

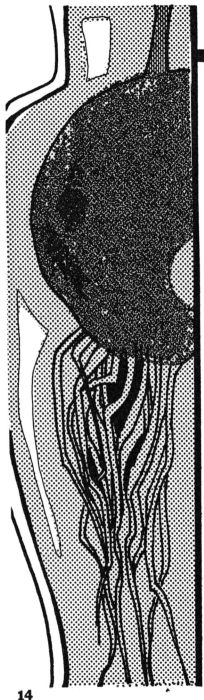

WHAT *IS* WRITING, ANYWAY?

You will be finding my own convictions about writing sprinkled throughout this book; and you won't have to search too hard for them! To share them boldly, I've had them underlined, and labeled each: BIAS—which is just what it is—a strongly held personal belief about some area of the writing process.

> ### BIAS #1 LIFE IS THE "STUFF" OF POETRY
> *Writing involves kids with the REAL happenings of their minds and worlds and hearts. They MUST be able to connect their writing to their lives: to communicate with words that are created by REAL feelings—NOT just by those which are comfortable for teachers to accept.*

One of the best lessons I ever learned about writing was taught me by a usually-quiet-and-teacher-pleasing nine-year old. I'd been "gently pushing" Kim for at least a dozen writing lessons, but she would sit with a blank paper (and a blanker expression) and insist, "I don't have anything to say." I was SURE she was capable, and one day my patience escaped me. I blurted, "Well, when ARE you going to write something?" Her almost inaudible answer came: "When you ask us to write about something that matters."

Oooo, that one hurt! She was right. I had concentrated ONLY on the happy and light and beautiful. In so doing, I had come close to insulting my students by acting as if strong human feelings—hurts and fears and frustrations and ecstacies—didn't exist for nine-year olds.

Now I know better. I know that when kids feel their opinions and real thoughts and wildest ideas are not going to be received with acceptance, then a whole part of themselves—that FORCE which creates poems and protests and questions and fantasies—will, at best, linger underground and, at worst, wither. But I know, too, that when humans find approval and acceptance for telling what's in their heads and hearts and dreams . . . AND are given the tools to tell it precisely and fluently . . . THEN . . .

> . . . communication satisfying to human needs flourishes.

> . . . respect for the technical skills of expression grows.

> . . . creative thinking flowers.

> . . . self-awareness, self-acceptance, self-significance bloom.

AND that kind of writing has little to do with "What I Did on My Summer Vacation."

AND that's why I'm SO sold on the need to get kids (and grownups) writing.

AND that's the focus of the ideas in these pages: giving kids the freedom, the support and the tools to let their voices be heard.

> **BIAS #2 IT'S BIGGER THAN YOU THINK**
>
> "Writing" is NOT synonymous with "stories" or "essays" or "themes" There are dozens of kinds of literature—some long, some very short—with which kids should have contact AND which they should write.

When you hear: "writing in the classroom," of what do you think? I used to define writing in pretty narrow terms. My repertoire was limited to stories, short poetry forms and some free verse—with maybe a myth or tall tale sprinkled in once or twice a year.

Last summer I asked a group of teachers to make a list of all the kinds of writing they had done in the past two weeks. After a half-hour we sat back in awe at the length of the list (over a hundred!) and at the variety of necessary writing tasks involved in everyday living. (Incidentally, not one person listed "stories" or "poems" or "essays" or several of the other things we assign in school.)

RIGHT NOW—before you read another sentence . . . . . or even before you blink or swallow or do ANYTHING ELSE—

STOP

turn to the next page—and look at the list of over two hundred kinds of written forms that your students can be trying.

THEN

. . . add your own ideas to the list.

. . . ask your students to expand the list.

. . . make a copy of those two pages and tape it to your desk.

. . . raise your right hand and vow to try at least thirty different kinds of writing during the school year. (Put a check by those . . . match them to units you're teaching . . . label each with the month you plan to use it.)

I certainly hope that you won't drop story-writing from your classroom . . . but, the next time you think, "writing," please think in terms of ANY form of communication that involves the written word. (And remember, you're teaching kids to LIVE—so include forms and topics that touch on a variety of the feelings and experiences of LIFE.)

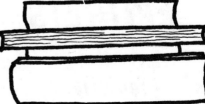

lyrics

catalog entries

POST SCRIPTS

gags

dialogues

jingles

mistrakes

KOANS

EPITHETS

predictions

INSTEAD OF, "WRITE A STORY," TRY . . . . . .

ads (for magazines
    newspapers
    yellow pages)
advice columns
allegories
anecdotes
announcements
anthems
appendices
apologies
assumptions
autobiographies
awards

ballads
beauty tips
bedtime stories
beginnings
billboards
biographies
blurbs
books
book jackets
book reviews
brochures
bulletins
bumper stickers

calendar quips
calorie charts
campaign speeches
cartoons
captions
cereal boxes
certificates
character sketches
church bulletins
community bulletins
couplets
comparisons

comic strips
complaints
constitutions
contracts
conundrums
conversations
critiques
cumulative stories

data sheets
definitions
descriptions
diaries
diets
directions
directories
documents
doubletalk
dramas
dream scripts

editorials
epilogues
epitaphs
encyclopedia entries
endings
essays
evaluations
exaggerations
exclamations
explanations

fables
fairy tales
fantasies
fashion articles
fashion show scripts
folklore
fortunes

game rules
graffiti
good news-bad news
greeting cards
grocery lists
gossip

headlines
horoscopes
how-to-do-it speeches

impromptu speeches
indexes
inquiries
insults
interviews
introductions (to people
    places
    books)
invitations

job applications
jokes
journals
jump rope rhymes

labels
legends
letters
lies
lists
love notes
luscious words
lyrics

magazines
marquee notices
memories
metaphors
menus

monologues
movie reviews
movie scripts
mysteries
myths

news analyses
newscasts
newspapers
nonsense
notebooks
nursery rhymes

obituaries
observations
odes
opinions

palindromes
pamphlets
parodies
party tips
persuasive letters
phrases
plays
poems
post cards
posters
prayers
problems
problem solutions
proformas
profound sayings
prologues
proposals
propaganda sheets
protest signs
protest letters
product descriptions
proverbs
puppet shows
puns
puzzles

quips
quizzes
questionnaires
questions
quotations

ransom notes
reactions
real estate notices
rebuttals
recipes
record covers
remedies
reports
requests
requiems
requisitions
resumes
reviews
revisions
riddles

sale notices
sales pitches
satires
schedules
secrets
self descriptions
sentences
sequels
serialized stories
sermons
signs
silly sayings
skywriting messages
slogans
soap operas
society news
songs
speeches
spoofs

spook stories
spoonerisms
sports accounts
sports analyses
superstitions

TV commercials
TV guides
TV programs
tall tales
telegrams
telephone directories
textbooks
thank you notes
theater programs
titles
tongue twisters
traffic rules
transcripts
travel folders
travel posters
tributes
trivia

used car descriptions

vignettes
vitas

want ads
wanted posters
warnings
wills
wise sayings
wishes
weather reports
weather forecasts
WORDS

yarns
yellow pages

crossword puzzles

PARABLES

codes

malapropisms

answers

BLOOPERS

hymns

rhyMes

paragraphs

Prophecy

19

WHY BOTHER?

Do you plan periods for writing—and then find the time has slithered by—or end up using it for finishing other things? Do you schedule writing experiences as religiously as you schedule math or reading or science?

Maybe you can identify with me when I admit that I'm not pleased about the times I let writing slide

> . . . OR the times I planned it so late in the day that everyone was low on energy, creativity and interest

> . . . OR the times I sandwiched it so tightly between music and recess that nobody had time to think, let alone write!

More writing-with-kids experiences have convinced me of the worth of the endeavor. More and more I TAKE the time. I hope to serve as a "prodder" for you because of the benefits which result when teachers bother to make time for writing. Again and again, in classrooms and homes where there is a commitment to a planned-and-consistent-offering-of-writing-sessions instead of a now-and-then-let's-write-a-story-if-there's-time approach, I see good things happening to kids.

Here are some of those GOOD REASONS for bothering:

1. Sensitivities to everyday, ordinary experiences are unlocked.

2. Writing heightens awarenesses of the people, the feelings, the comedy, the tragedy, the ridiculous, the REAL in their environments.

3. Kids begin to look at common things in uncommon ways.... and imagination mushrooms.

4. They grow in awe of the POWER and BEAUTY of WORDS, and begin to see their language as an instrument of many talents.

5. In writing and sharing, kids discover the POTENCY and AC-CEPTABILITY of feelings.

6. The creative processes are challenged and strengthened .... flexible and original thinking flourishes.

7. Involvement with literature increases. Interest in reading their own and each other's writing spreads to all kinds of written materials.

8. Writing gives an outlet for sharing the wildest notions, the most astounding discoveries, highly treasured secrets and outlandish hypotheses.

9. Writing lets kids in on the pleasure that comes from playing with words .... and turns them on to the pure enjoyment of the rhythms and sounds of their language.

10. The writing climate fosters mental health and appreciation of other persons.

GETTING AROUND TO IT

Somehow the day or the period was never quite long enough for everything I'd intended to fit into it. And even on the days when I conscientiously reserved an hour, I had to deal with the "not-every-one-feels-creative-from-1:00-to-2:00-on-Tuesday-afternoons" reality. (Sometimes NO one felt inspired, including me!)

If you're having trouble getting around to writing, or if you're bored with too rigid a writing schedule, these ten FINDING THE TIME YOU DIDN'T KNOW YOU HAD tips may help you:

1. Sneak "creative" writing into your language skills lessons.

2. Sneak technical writing skills into your creative writing lessons.

   (More on how to do both the above in Chapter 5.)

3. Mix writing in with a math lesson, a social science project, a science experiment, a musical listening session, a physical exercise break, a story hour, an art experience or a library trip.

   (Loads of ideas for this are found in Chapter 8.)

4. Ask the kids to collect "winter phrases" at recess or "crunchy words" at lunch or "creepy sayings" in their dark basements.

   (The groundwork is started before they even get to class.)

5. Use short bits of time for short or pre-writing exercises:

   > the first 10 minutes in the morning
   > the 12 minutes of cooling-off time after gym
   > the 3 minutes before the bell rings
   > the time you're waiting in line for the assembly
   > the 15 minutes before you go to get class pictures taken

   (For short writing and word play activities galore, see Chapter 2.)

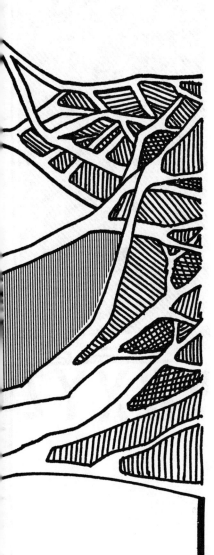

6. Write at a different TIME each day (or week):

early morning when kids are fresh
late afternoon when kids are "wearing down"
before lunch when they're hungry
after lunch when they're full
before gym when they're restless
after gym when they're tired
the first half of the period
the last half of the period
the middle 15 minutes of the period
the WHOLE period

(The variety keeps writing interesting AND increases the chances for touching on different feelings, moods, ideas and discoveries.)

7. Do it a different WAY each time:

orally	in writing
quickly	taking a long time
independently	together
in small groups	as a whole group
with re-writing	without re-writing
with the teacher	without the teacher
inside	outside
in centers	in private journals
at school	at home

8. One day a month, skip math—and use the time for writing.

9. Take a WHOLE afternoon or a WHOLE period for JUST WRITING.

10. Break it up into segments:

Day 1	(10 min.)	Do a dance to motivate thinking.
Day 2	(10 min.)	Brainstorm together words to describe the dancing experience. Record the ideas.
Day 3	(10 min.)	Combine words from list into phrases.
Day 4	(15 min.)	Split into pairs and choose 4 phrases to combine into a few lines for a song.
Day 5	(15 min.)	Form a small group to arrange lines into complete song lyrics. Make a large copy.
Day 6	(15 min.)	Choose or create a tune for the lyrics.
Day 7	(15 min.)	Rehearse and record song as a group.

THE CLIMATE WHERE KIDS WILL DARE TO WRITE

> ### BIAS #3 COMFORT IS THE KEY
> *The valve that opens fluent, effective communication is an environment where persons can risk exposing their REAL lives: where the act of telling what one is really feeling and thinking is treated with utmost respect.*

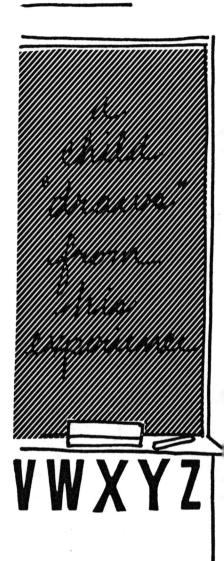

In such an environment, there is:

* ACCEPTANCE . . . . of selves . . . of individuals . . . of ideas . . . of differences

> *The climate says to kids, "YOU ARE VALUED."*

* OPEN COMMUNICATION . . . . caring . . . love . . . warmth . . . support . . . . AND plenty of "straight talk" about things that matter

> *The climate says, "YOU ARE IMPORTANT ENOUGH TO LISTEN TO," and, "I CARE ENOUGH TO TELL YOU ABOUT ME, TOO."*

* FREEDOM . . . . to try . . . to risk . . . to question . . . to think unconventional thoughts . . . to fantasize . . . to explore . . . to be honest

> *The climate says, "IT'S OKAY TO BE YOURSELF AND TO BE SPONTANEOUS."*

* ABSENCE OF STRESS . . . . freedom from value judgments . . . from criticism . . . from over-analysis . . . from comparison . . . from competition

> *The climate says:*
>
> *"YOUR THOUGHTS HAVE PRECEDENCE OVER MECHANICS."*
>
> *"THE INNER POETRY OF YOUR DAYDREAMS IS RESPECTED."*
>
> *"YOUR WILD IMAGININGS AND INVENTIONS THAT DEFY LAWS ARE PRIZED."*

* SERIOUSNESS . . . . about the hard work and discipline involved . . . about the BALANCE between the FREEDOM to imagine and doodle and experiment with ideas and play with words and explore relationships and let thoughts flow—and the DISCIPLINE of meeting deadlines and making alterations and producing a clear, precise final copy in language that communicates

> *The climate says, "WRITING IS FUN, BUT IT'S ALSO WORK."*

* A BOTTOMLESS BARREL OF STIMULATION . . . . loads of fresh ideas

> *The climate says, "YOUR INSIDE AND OUTSIDE WORLDS ARE FULL OF THOUGHTS AND PEOPLE AND HAPPENINGS THAT ARE WORTHY SUBJECTS FOR WRITING."*

HOW TO BUILD THE CLIMATE

Obviously, such a setting takes time and work to build, as you well know—those of you who work each year at creating a happy learning community with a new group of students. You don't just walk in the first day and say, "Look, kids, I'm a nice person—you can trust me!" It's a little bit like love: you don't convince someone you love him or her by saying it over and over. It takes months—sometimes years—of behaving in loving ways for you to be believed.

There are some steps teachers can take to hasten the development of a comfortable "home" for writing growth. You can

*   SHARE YOUR OWN EXCITEMENT ABOUT WRITING. Your eagerness can spark theirs!

*   RESPECT THE WRITTEN WORD. Share and enjoy freely with children ALL kinds of literature.

*   REMOVE OBSTACLES TO WRITING. Competition, restrictive or dull forms, rhyme, comparison, over-analysis and fill-in-the-blank-with-one-answer sheets often choke out fluent writing.

*   ENCOURAGE CAREFREE INVENTIVENESS. A person can't create a brand new thing unless he/she feels free to do something nobody expects.

*   PROVIDE PLENTY OF TIME. Writers need time for thinking, writing, trying, re-writing, changing, sharing. Many of the freshest thoughts appear after toying with several.

*   LET THEM WRITE WITHOUT STOPPING TO CORRECT. Good ideas come faster than you can write—and you can rarely re-capture one once it's lost. You can ALWAYS go back and fix spelling or edit.

*   WRITE TOGETHER . . . OFTEN. Collaborative writing keeps the momentum going, eases discomfort for reluctant writers and builds togetherness.

*   PROVIDE DIRECTIONS THAT CHALLENGE. Don't be afraid to suggest a direction. All of us need that from time to time! Just make sure you choose something that matters to kids.

*   ALWAYS, ALWAYS SHARE. The importance you attach to their writing is the importance kids will attach to theirs and others'.

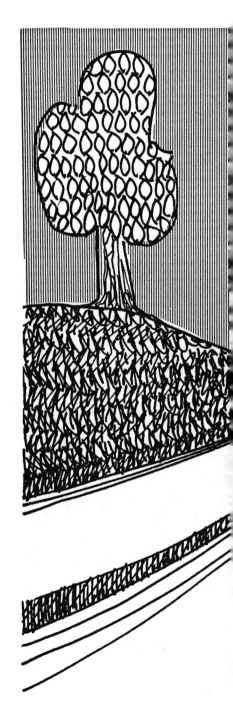

> **BIAS #4 THE TEACHER IS THE DIFFERENCE**
>
> *The teacher's enthusiasm is the #1 motivator of writing; the teacher's love for words and literature is contagious. And the open student-teacher relationship is the soil for writing growth. Every child should have the chance to write alongside an adult who enjoys the process.*

I doubt that any one person can actually TEACH another to write. As teachers, we can only

   . . . unleash the forces of expression.

   . . . awaken sensitivities to selves and others.

   . . . stir responses to ideas and events.

   . . . prod awarenesses of feelings and sensations.

   . . . offer forms and tools for combining words.

That's quite a responsibility, isn't it? A "special" person in that "teacher spot" becomes a major force in the setting of that dare-to-write climate. I don't know how that makes YOU feel, but I do know that I need reminders and checkpoints for myself—to give me direction in "setting the tone" and to "keep me on my toes."

So I am sharing with you my own AM I READY? checklist. I look at it often in the beginning of the year, and dig it out at least once a month after that. (This helps in creating a warm human climate that affects ALL areas of community living!) You're free to copy this so that you can have it handy as often as you need it.

AM I READY?   A TEACHER CHECKLIST

_____ I consistently find and use fresh ideas for writing.

_____ I listen—REALLY listen—to my kids.

_____ I allow expression of ALL emotions (and receive them without being shocked).

_____ I write WITH my kids and enjoy it.

_____ I fiercely protect kids' privacy and honor their confidences.

_____ I show individuals that they are valued.

_____ I share MY writing with my students.

_____ I am serious about the importance of writing.

_____ I express my SELF freely to my students (tell about my dreams and fears and disappointments and ideas).

_____ I don't hide from kids the truth about the some-times-pain of writing.

_____ I refrain from comparing one student's writing to another's.

_____ I can accept that every student will NOT be turned on by every writing experience I plan.

Children, there are words
pasted to the undersides of leaves
that match
your secrets.

                Disorderly,
      full of dragons
and butterflies
              and sharks
pretending to be snowclouds
in September.

                Let the long beautiful ones hang
                off the edges of your paper.

And what if
you stuck them in store windows
with no price tags
              and put them on menus
              like specials

And what if
you stuck them into paper airplanes and sailed them
into India
or buried them under the begonias

And what if
you got up a parade
with some people playing cash registers
and everybody singing the poets' National Anthem

and making up their own
veined words.
                    Daniel Lusk

2

"My kids say they can't think of anything to write."

FOUNDATION

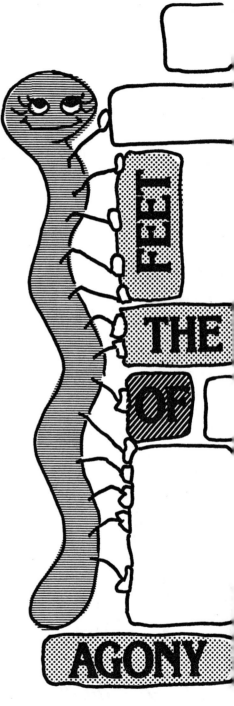

> ### BIAS #5 LOVE OF LANGUAGE IS INBORN
>
> *The sounds and rhythms and melodies of words are pleasing to young minds and ears. From birth, children respond with delight to language.*

Just watch a group of young children enjoying the alliteration of "Peter Piper picked a peck of pickled peppers" or the rhythm of "Not by the hair of your chinny-chin-chin," and, if you're not convinced already of the NATURAL appeal of language, you will be. To be reminded of that, I need only observe Scotty, my two-year-old neighbor, marching about my yard chanting, "caterpillar, caterpillar," or hear him endlessly repeating his favorite phrase—"zucchini tetrazzini"—experimenting with its sound at various pitches and paces.

> ### BIAS #6 CHILDREN ARE FULL OF POETRY
>
> *Children's minds (even very young ones) create beautiful and sensitive combinations of words. In their efforts to explain their ever-new world with limited vocabularies, they often speak in complex metaphors.*

Smashed Potatoes by Jane Martel is a delightful collection of recipes dictated by children too young to write to an adult who transcribed them without alteration. (See bibliography in Chapter 9.) It illustrates potently the poetic nature of the language of the young; it is filled with phrases such as:

"Use red meat balls and the soapy kind of cheese that tastes a little bit rotten."
"Put them in a skillet pan on the biggest black circle on the roof of your stove."
"Mix the sauce in a blender so your elbows don't hurt."
"... put every single thing you have in a mother-size pan."
"Fringe up the lettuce in little heaps in all the bowls."

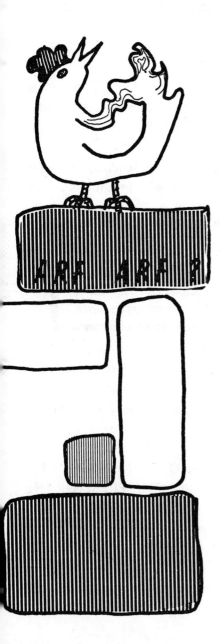

When Krista, my niece, began talking, I started keeping a list of her original metaphors. Among my favorites are her exclamation the first morning of arising to the sound of newly-acquired chickens: "Mommy, the chickens are barking!" and her explanation when she saw my husband coming up the driveway on crutches with a new whole-leg cast: "Look Aunt Marge, Uncle Doug is swinging on wishbones!"

Isn't it amusing (and a little sad, too) that a four-year old who doesn't know the word "burner" generates "the biggest black circle on the roof of your stove," and then, when she gets to fourth grade, we plan writing lessons to help her forget the word and say it in a novel way? Let's try to keep her metaphors flowing AFTER she enters school, and on into adulthood!

As we begin a chapter on the foundations of writing, I share these biases about the NATURAL abilities of children in order to encourage you to BELIEVE that the inner poetry exists. So many times I set out to write with kids holding on to expectations far too low, because I forget just that. Thinking back to Scotty and Krista and *Smashed Potatoes* helps me keep sight of the real possibilities!

I don't really think you'll have to TEACH your students to love language—but you may have to BRING THEM BACK to words, especially if they're no longer young and free with expression. By taking advantage of the natural fascination with words, you CAN help to bring alive that pleasure—and turn it into a creative force. This chapter of word-play activities and short writing exercises will help you do that—enjoyably!

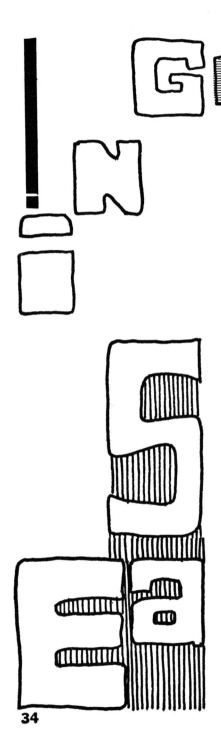

EASING INTO WRITING . . . FOUR TIPS

Even confident writers sometimes feel pangs of discomfort at the sound of "Write a . . . " Here are some reminders to help ease those pangs and get writers started . . . comfortably:

1. GET KIDS TALKING . . . about dreams or schemes or people or sounds or feelings or social issues or wild inventions . . . or anything!

    > *BIAS #7 WHAT YOU CAN SAY, YOU CAN WRITE*
    > *Creative talking is a stimulus to creative writing. If kids can communicate orally, teachers can use that to convince them that they DO have something to write.*

    If a student thinks she CAN'T write, start with what she CAN do; often the CAN is speaking. Therefore, many of the activities of this chapter are ORAL experiences (although they may be written, too) designed to get communication flowing and to build the I CAN feeling.

2. BE CAREFUL NOT TO CHOKE OFF EXPRESSION OR LIMIT THINKING BY THE WAY YOU PRESENT THE ASSIGNMENT OR RESPOND TO THE IDEAS.
    Sometimes we say too much or give so many examples of one kind that our students hear the message, "This is what the teacher wants," instead of, "What are all the possibilities?" Begin these word-play activities in ways that leave open options for many directions.

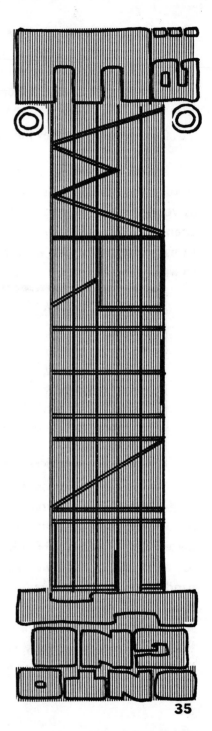

3. EXPRESS <u>YOURSELF</u> ... FREELY!

The teacher IS the difference, remember? Talk about your wild ideas. Make public your embarrassing moments, your fondest memories, your secret desires, your most haunting fears. A teacher's honesty is a very effective opener for students' bottled up notions and feelings. When you use the exercises in this chapter, make sure YOU contribute your ideas too.

4. START WITH SHORT, FUN, NON-THREATENING BITS OF WRITING.

This chapter is full of them!

By SHORT, I mean exercises that fit into small segments of time and end without being over-worked or dragged on until someone gets bored.

By FUN, I mean possibilities with strong kid-appeal: suggestions that challenge thinking, move along snappily, get them involved immediately and capitalize on the natural attractions to words.

By NON-THREATENING, I mean tasks that assure success for every writer or that sneak kids into writing without the fearsome anticipation of a "formal writing assignment."

WORD PLAY *IS* CHILD'S PLAY ... AND THAT'S NOT ALL

Words have so many surprising talents!

... Some amaze and excite and enchant you.

... Others set up wonderful vibrations in your ears.

... Others frighten or bewilder or disappoint.

... Some feel absolutely delicious on your tongue.

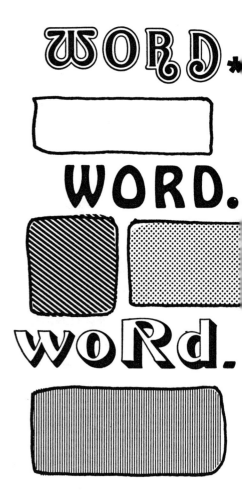

I am a word-lover ... one who is fascinated by the POWER of words. And I believe kids should experience the magic of words. Just as young bodies are developed by physical play, so young minds are strengthened by verbal play; and since words are the base units of verbal expression, frolic with them serves as an important forerunner to writing in any form.

> *BIAS #8   EVERYBODY NEEDS TO PLAY WITH WORDS*
>
> *Word play should never end. ALL writers—young, old, new, experienced, enthusiastic, lazy, struggling, gifted —need to go back and romp with words: to keep alive the appreciation of language, to strengthen the roots of expression, to learn new words and usages, to expand minds.*

You may be thinking that the word-play and short writing ideas of this chapter are for young or slow writers. You might see them as pre-writing exercises to use until students are ready for the longer pieces. BUT THESE ARE REAL WRITING, TOO! Short writing is for all of us ... and we should do it often! Surely, new writers, handicapped writers and reluctant writers will need lots of word play, but even advanced writers (including YOU) need to return often to such exercises to build confidence and sophistication. Don't forget that the foundation of any structure needs to be kept strong. And WORDS are major building blocks in the foundation of written communication.

As you choose ideas from the remaining pages of this chapter, keep in mind that they may be used in a variety of ways to meet a variety of your needs. In most cases you can use the activity

. . . during a 5-10 minute (or shorter) time slot

OR . . . for a full writing period

. . . orally, with everyone contributing ideas

OR . . . in writing, with students recording the lists, words, etc.

OR . . . some of each within one period

. . . together, in collaboration

OR . . . in small groups, as partners, in trios

OR . . . alone, as an individual assignment

. . . just one time as a motivator or review

OR . . . repeated at several points throughout the year, adding depth and sophistication each time

. . . just as each is described

OR . . . as the basis for a longer writing assignment

For example: You may return to use the impressions collected in your WORD TASTING PARTY as the raw material for poems or menus.

. . . as it is, if it suits your kids' level

OR . . . with adaptation (simplified or elaborated)

The HOW TO ADAPT A GOOD IDEA section at the end of this chapter will give you some examples of such adaptations.

Read some of these words to your kids . . . and LISTEN to them .   one at a time. Then collect words JUST FOR THEIR SOUNDS! Say some of them over and over.

abracadabra	*ghosts*	*lazy*	*tremulous*
giggle	*whoosh*	*provocative*	*cinnamon*
gypsy	*quince*	*goggles*	*buzz*
grumble	*cornucopia*	*caterpillar*	*eucalyptus*
slippery	*trickery*	*murmur*	*banana*
sassafrass	*whisper*	*sesame*	*sultry*
shiver	*marshmallow*	*sycamore*	*ginger*
galoshes	*sneezes*	*gazebo*	*pirouette*
whistle	*smithereens*	*bamboozle*	*frangipani*

40

. . . . THEN COLLECT!

Build lists of words for special purposes. These can be started in spare moments—then added to as the year goes along. NEXT, start a class word book. Every classroom needs one. Include a page of:

people words	*city words*	*country words*
loud words	*soft words*	*gentle words*
outdoor words	*grumpy words*	*color words*
wet words	*odd words*	*busy words*
public words	*private words*	*tasting words*
harsh words	*indoor words*	*joyful words*
bewitching words	*dry words*	*silly words*
lazy words	*convincing words*	*hurried words*
serious words	*frivolous words*	*conceited words*

The kinds of words you collect will depend upon the needs of your group. Use the collections again and again as raw material for writing during the year.

> *For example: When Julie gets stuck for ideas for her character sketch, you can send her to get the "people words" page—or when Tim needs some specific descriptive words for his city poem, he can take the "city words" to his desk.*

WORD WHEELS

In the hub of a cardboard wheel, write a word which is over-used in children's writing ("pretty," "said," "ate," "went," etc.) Ask kids to fill the spokes of the wheel with alternate ways of saying the word. THEN . . . keep the wheels in sight as helpers for writers-in-need-of-ideas. Post them on a wall or tack them flat on the ceiling and you'll have a permanent thesaurus-at-a-glance all year long.

ways to fool around

WORDS CAN MAKE YOU SICK

Think of words that, when you say them, might make someone feel:

frightened	angry	sick	thirsty
cold	warm	nervous	wet
lazy	sad	worried	in a hurry
surprised	silly	slow	lonely
hurt	confused	hungry	like laughing

with words...

START WITH 15

As a group . . compile a list of 15 words that students like—ANY words:

aqua	snooze	cinnamon
icicle	scratching	abracadabra
silvery	buttery	sunset
explodes	applesauce	shadows
squirting	polka-dotted	giraffe

Then, ask each to combine any 3 words into a phrase. They may later combine these short phrases into longer phrases and sentences.

* a buttery, cinnamon sunset
* cinnamon applesauce explodes
* At sunset shadows snooze.

* Abracadabra! An aqua icicle!
* scratching, squirting shadows
* The giraffe's neck is a polka-dotted icicle.

BABY TEETH ARE DROP-OUTS

Share some puns with students. Let them create their own or collect them from other sources. Keep a PUN notebook, hang them on a clothesline or fill a graffiti mural with puns.

A nervous mosquito is a jitterbug.
Gravity will let you down.
A talking dog is smarter than a spelling bee.
Custer wore Arrow Shirts!
Radar cops study speed reading.

BEAUTY CONTESTS

Choose words to be contestants in a "beauty" contest. Kids can compose posters, banners, slogans, buttons and speeches to convince others to vote for their words.

THE GAME OF THE NAME

For each letter of your name write a word that is part of a newspaper headline or of a story title or sign:

Martian	*Astronaut*	*Rejects*	*Greasy*	*Eggs*
Beware		*Eccentric*	*Violinist!*	
Alligators	*Never*	*Need*	*Education*	

Later they might go back and actually write the story or article.

PALINDROMES

Collect words that read the same forwards as backwards:

pop	*mom*	*noon*	*pup*	*level*	*gag*
dad	*radar*	*to t*	*refer*	*rotor*	*kayak*

Phrases and sentences can be palindromes, too. Try some:

evil olive   *not a ton*   *a toyota*
wet stew   *too hot to hoot*   *pot top*
          Was it a cat I saw?   *Madam, I'm Adam!*

SASSY SARAH, SITTING SIDEWAYS, CITED SIXTEEN SILLY STANZAS

Create alliterative sentences by starting every word with the same sound. Pass one around a circle, with each student adding a word. Or, let kids make them up by themselves. Keep the dictionaries handy for finding words!

Which witch wished whammies on whales?
Sam sifted sand in Suzie's sneakers.
Cross camels crammed creamed croutons clumsily.

MAIL-A-WHALE?

Where would you mail a whale?
Here's a letter my goat wrote.
I'd like to see a possum blossom.
Don't ever shake a rake at a snake.
Should you jump rope with a pope?

These are a challenge for older kids—and great fun for little kids. Make up some of your own —and illustrate them!

CONVERSATION STOPPERS

Think of sentences which, if said at the dinner table, would be guaranteed to stop the conversation and make people listen:
Mom, did you tell dad about the car?
I wonder if Jimmy ever got out of that hole?
Dad, what's internal revenue? The man who called today said he was from there.

MY DENTIST BORES ME TO TEARS

Try to hold a conversation full of "occupational puns":
"By gum, I hear you went to the dentist today."
"Yes, it was quite a filling experience."
"Did you meet the new hygienist, named Floss?"
"Definitely—I found her to be captivating!"
Here's another start:
"My mother says it's a drain on our budget to hire a plumber."

YOURS TILL THE BUTTER FLIES

Add to this list of good endings . . . .
> *Yours till Niagara Falls,*
> *Yours till the door stops,*
> *Yours till the ocean waves,*

TEAKETTLE

A game with homophones. One person says a sentence in which two or more homophones are replaced by the word "teakettle." Can you solve this one?

> *I Teakettle an ocean liner sailing on the blue Teakettle.*
> *(I see an ocean liner sailing on the blue sea.)*

If you have an old teapot, get kids to fill it with pairs of homophones. Then they can take turns drawing a pair when there's a spare moment for the game.

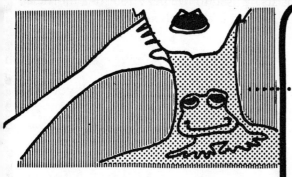

IDIOMS DRIVE ME CRAZY

Start a list of idioms such as:
> *I'm tickled pink.*
> *She has a frog in her throat.*
> *We had the minister for lunch.*
> *If you break that, I'll crown you!*

Turn kids on to listening for them at home, on TV, in school —anywhere. Start making up your own, too!

WHAT'S OUR BAG?

Take turns putting "secret" objects into a bag. Each student writes a related word on the bag after he's peeked in. Later, use the bags with their word lists for writing "What Am I?" riddles. OR— —classmates can try to guess what's in the bag after someone orally supplies words as clues. But they may only guess by asking if other words apply: i.e.: *"Is it buoyant?"*

ADVENTURES IN SENSITIVITY

To give kids an idea of the many words available for communicating one idea, and to illustrate the slight differences in meaning of synonyms, ask them to find words that could be used to describe beauty.

For example:

a sunset might be	*magnificent, vivid*
a hilltop view	*breath-taking, awesome*
a new car	*sleek, elegant*
a kitten	*cute, adorable*
a forest	*lush, stately*
a woman	*lovely, gorgeous, chic*
a mountain	*majestic*
a building	*splendid*
a cake	*luscious*
a piece of jewelry	*exquisite*

YOU NAME IT!

Did you hear about the plumber named "Seymour Pipes" and his partner "Duane A. Tubb"? My sister-in-law has gone for oral surgery to "Dr. Slaughter" and a friend insists he used to live next door to a mortician named "I. C. Stiphs." (Do you believe that one?) Anyway, it's fun and brain-stretching to make up names for persons or animals. What would you name:

an elephant? . . . twins? . . . a huge dog? . . . a clown? . . . a telephone repair person?
a skydiver? . . . an exterminator? . . . a tree surgeon? . . . a crossing guard?

I've seen a fabric shop called "Nip and Tuck" and a pet food store named "The Cat's Meow." Ask your kids to name business establishments such as:

a waffle house . . . a water bed store . . . a heart surgeon's office . . . a wig boutique . . .
a rock shop . . . a washing machine repair service . . .

VERBAL GYMNASTICS

Choose some words or short phrases with differing rhythms. Have kids march or drum or stretch to the rhythm of each word. Try:

elevator operator
elephantiasis
banana, banana, banana

Go on to longer sentences. Ask individuals or groups to make up exercises to fit the rhythms—and teach them to the class.

WHAT'S MISSING?

Find the one word that completes the other four in each group:

up	roar	stairs	set	seven
back	ward	quarter	ache	side
fly	horse	ball	gad	swatter
chese	cake	cottage	cloth	blue
gate	way	garden	water	post
down	goose	first	town	stairs
ship	mate	friend	shape	member
dust	gold	pan	storm	mop
drum	hum	ear	corps	beat
thumb	nail	green	tack	tom
moon	stone	harvest	shine	blue

BLOOPERS

Also known as "spoonerisms," these are mixed up phrases such as: *"Pardon me, miss, your ship is slowing."* and *"Who milled the spilk?"* and *"I want creaches and peam on my cereal."* Make some bloopers of your own. Ask your kids to try whole paragraphs full of bloopers. P.S. *I'm not as dumb as some thinkle peep I am!*

WORD TASTING

About mid-way through the morning, give students apples (or celery, carrots, granola). Ask them to say or write a word as you direct:

Write a word that tells something about how your apple looks.
Write a word that tells about how your apple feels.
Take a bite—write a sound word. How does it sound when you bite in?
Write a word that tells how it feels in your mouth.
Write a taste word.
Write a word that tells how it feels when you swallow.
Write an aftertaste word.
Finish this: The girl next to me chewing on her apple sounds like _____
    or Eating apples reminds me of _____
    or This celery is as crunchy as _____
Can you think of a person who reminds you of an apple? Write:
        _____ is like an apple because _____

43

WOULD A LAPIDARY PLAY LEAPFROG IN A LYCEUM?

A dictionary exercise that teaches words in a way kids will remember!

1. Could a GARGOYLE gargle?
2. Are you PARSIMONIOUS?
3. Do you like your PHYSIOGNOMY?
4. Where does a COWLICK reside?
5. Would you climb into a MAW?
6. Does a waffle have a WATTLE?
7. Would a BARNACLE wear a MONOCLE?
8. Name two things that are MUCILAGINOUS.
9. Would you ask a GAMMON to dance with you?
10. Is the fat lady at the circus likely to be SVELTE?
11. Do you know anyone who is FASTIDIOUS?
12. Could you put ice cream into a CALABASH?
13. Do you think an OBELISK would make a good pet?
14. How could a VECTOR be harmful to a RECTOR?
15. Would a LAPIDARY play leapfrog in a LYCEUM?
16. Would you expect to find a UVULA in an orchestra?
17. Is a boy's first violin lesson likely to be EUPHONIOUS?
18. If you're going to meet a TYCOON, would you take an umbrella?
19. Might you get arrested if you try to ABET a crime?
20. Which is more valuable to your mother, her SPATULA or SCAPULA?
21. When was the last time you were accused of being OBSTREPEROUS?
22. Which is more SANGUINARY, a vampire or a VERANDAH?

44

DILLY DEFINITIONS

Give kids a word they do NOT know. Ask them to write a definition for it. (OR they may choose their own unknowns from a dictionary.) Then, enjoy sharing the new meanings before you compare them to the actual definitions. You might choose words that you want the students to be learning anyway.

Try:

copacetic	quaggle	siluroid
tigon	termagant	garbulent
amok	mome	pruinose
syllabub		

(You may use some made-up words too!)

VOCABULARY PIN-UPS

When you're anxious for kids to learn and remember vocabulary words, send them hunting for pictures that portray their words. The boy or girl who finds a tumbling pile of football players to match the word "chaos" will not be likely to forget its meaning.

OR

Start with the picture! Give one interesting picture to each student, and allow 2 days for learning a new word which in some way matches the picture.

DO-IT-YOURSELF WORDS

Have a session for creating original words. *Magniflubescent* isn't a real word—but it certainly should be! Kids can create words that are meaningful, useful and fun. Ask them to write their words in sentences, prepare dictionary entries, make up synonyms or brag about their originals.

nVENTAWORDinVENTAMEANINGiN

WORDS YOU'D LIKE TO KNOW

Present 4 or 5 new words to the class (or ask each student to choose a few from the dictionary that he doesn't know—without reading the definitions). Use the words in a poem or saying. Here are some finished poems:

A DROLL came down with JABORANDI
Her fever rose, her DRUIDS sank low.
Dr. VERDANT arrived and prescribed SCRUPLES
And said, "You'll be well in a MEMENTO!"   Hilary, Grade 4

The frog croaked as he JADED from PLACID to PLACID
He stopped on a PROLOGUE to sip VERDANTLY from a pool of DIADEMS.   Christopher, Grade 3

Don't CORNICE me with KISSES
While I'm dancing the MACABRE.   Jenny, Grade 2

45

ALPHABET ANTICS

For each letter of the alphabet, try to write a word that fits into a particular category you've chosen. For example:

Words That Describe Children

Adventuresome	Noisy
Busy	Obedient
Curious	Polite
Delightful	Quick
Eager	Rambunctious
Frivolous	Sneaky
Generous	Tireless
Horrible	Useful
Ingenious	Vocal
Joyful	Wonderful
Kind	X-tra special
Lovable	Young
Mischievous	Zesty

Names of Animals

Alligator	Nuthatch
Butterfly	Opossum
Camel	Porcupine
Dinosaur	Quail
Elephant	Rattlesnake
Fox	Spider
Gorilla	Tiger
Hyena	Unicorn
Iguana	Viper
Jackal	Wolf
Koala	Xiphosuran
Llama	Yak
Mole	Zebra

TWISTED TONGUES

Read lots of tongue twisters to kids. Make up some of your own. (Words with lots of Ss and Zs and CH sounds work well.) Challenge students to make up whole tongue twisting sentences or stories.

Try saying these at least 5 times— — —fast!

a box of mixed biscuits   *Peggy Babcock*   *Wise Willy whistled Wednesday.*

HEADLINERS

Create original titles for news articles or dances or books or magazines or songs or movies or events.

What would you call a new reader for first graders?
...   *a song to be sung at a blueberry festival?*
...   *a banquet for zoo animals?*
...   *a book on how to give a haircut?*
...   *a new Halloween dance?*
...   *a theme song for a queen's coronation?*
...   *a movie about a mystery on the moon?*

It's challenging to ask the questions, too. And it's valuable to work with just ONE idea for a while—to see how many different titles can be invented.

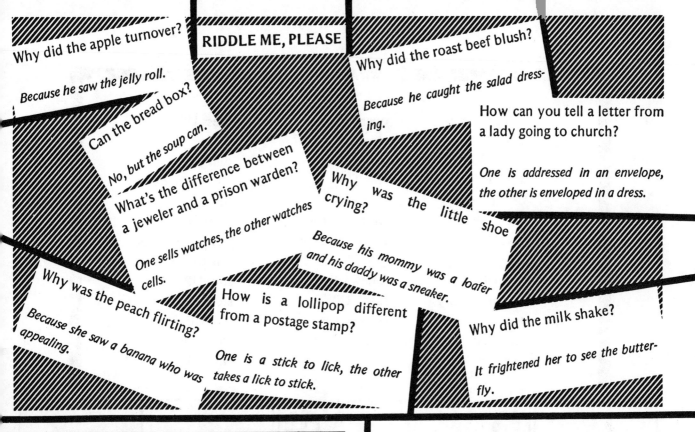

RIDDLE ME, PLEASE

Why did the apple turnover?

Because he saw the jelly roll.

Can the bread box?

No, but the soup can.

What's the difference between a jeweler and a prison warden?

One sells watches, the other watches cells.

Why was the peach flirting?

Because she saw a banana who was appealing.

Why did the roast beef blush?

Because he caught the salad dressing.

Why was the little shoe crying?

Because his mommy was a loafer and his daddy was a sneaker.

How is a lollipop different from a postage stamp?

One is a stick to lick, the other takes a lick to stick.

How can you tell a letter from a lady going to church?

One is addressed in an envelope, the other is enveloped in a dress.

Why did the milk shake?

It frightened her to see the butterfly.

WHAT DO YOU KNOW ABOUT A TREE?

With a partner, brainstorm all the words you can which are in any way related to trees. Allow the brainstorming to continue as long as ideas are flowing, then switch to a different topic. OR, collect the words you've shared and save them for a later writing exercise. In contributing your own words to the session, try to encourage divergent thinking:

wood — pencils — hollow — willow — forest — shade — sap — lightening — gnarled — seed — nest — petrified — paper, etc.

SENTENCE STRETCHING

Start with a short sentence or group of words. Pass it around to about 6 people, with the rule that each person must add or change ONE word to make the sentence more specific and more interesting:

She ate dinner.

became, for some first graders:

A hungry ballerina gobbled her sloppy green soup.

Sixth graders turned it into:

A ravenous sow slurped mush and slop with uncouth gulps.

47

WHAT'S UP?

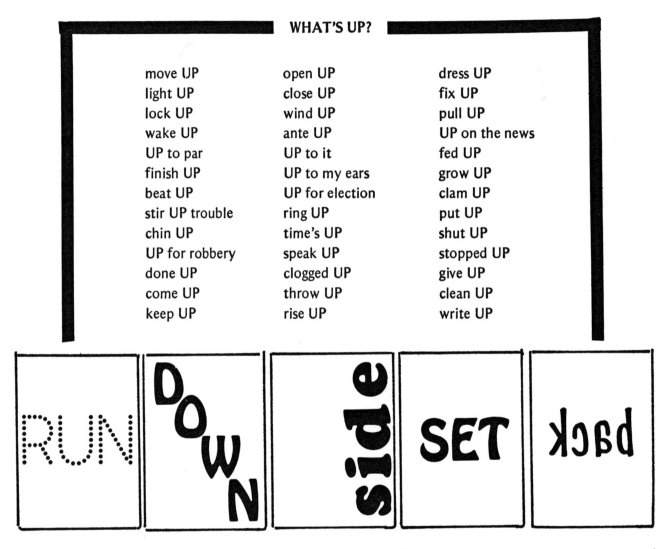

move UP	open UP	dress UP
light UP	close UP	fix UP
lock UP	wind UP	pull UP
wake UP	ante UP	UP on the news
UP to par	UP to it	fed UP
finish UP	UP to my ears	grow UP
beat UP	UP for election	clam UP
stir UP trouble	ring UP	put UP
chin UP	time's UP	shut UP
UP for robbery	speak UP	stopped UP
done UP	clogged UP	give UP
come UP	throw UP	clean UP
keep UP	rise UP	write UP

RUN DOWN side SET back

There are other words in our language that have so many uses (just look for the long dictionary entries): time . . . . . run . . . . . . down . . . . . . side . . . . . . set . . . . . . back . . . . . . Start collecting a list of the many uses of a little word, then ask students to work in groups or as a whole group to combine the uses into a story or poem or paragraph. Here is an OUT-story done by three fourth-graders.

You're OUTnumbered

For crying OUT loud, it sure is confusing trying to make sense OUT of all the ways to use the word OUT.

Before you're even OUT of diapers you learn that people can be OUT to lunch, start OUT on a trip, cry OUT with pain, dig OUT of a snowbank, turn OUT a cake, fade OUT of the picture, be OUT of style, give OUT compliments, back OUT of a deal, run OUT of money, behave OUT rageously, get Chinese food at a carry OUT, break OUT of jail, fake OUT other people, or dash OUT to the OUThouse.

When you first try to spin OUT on your tricycle and you wipe OUT—your mother can get OUT the dirt by washing it OUT or soaking it OUT or rubbing it OUT, and if none of those work, she can throw it OUT!

In school you find OUT fast not to get OUT of line. You're OUT of luck if you answer OUT of turn, because then the teacher won't let you OUT to recess until she bawls you OUT. And when you're OUT side playing softball, you hope you don't strike OUT. Don't get OUT of sorts with the umpire or you'll get kicked OUT.

When you grow up you learn that an OUT of sight chick is a knockOUT, and if she's OUT of your league, all you can do is eat your heart OUT. When you're old enough to go OUT on a date, you'll probably break OUT with pimples. You can take your date OUT to your favorite hangOUT—and if she doesn't want to make OUT, you'll feel down and OUT. Then you'll get OUT before you're left OUT in the cold.

Well, we're about OUT of our minds with this OUTlandish stuff, so we're going to cut OUT because we've run OUT........ Doug and Scott and Peter G.

WORD RUBBINGS

Cut letters from cardboard and/or textured materials. Create designs by placing paper over the letters and rubbing with charcoal, pencil or crayon.

WORD MOBILES

Hang letters from mobiles to form a word . . OR . . hang within one mobile several words related to one idea.

WORDS ARE WORKS OF ART

Ask students to create a picture or a design by repeating a word (or several words) in an interesting pattern.

WORD IMAGES

Fill a large piece of paper with the letters of one word. Make a design by filling in the spaces between the letters with color, shapes, lines, etc.

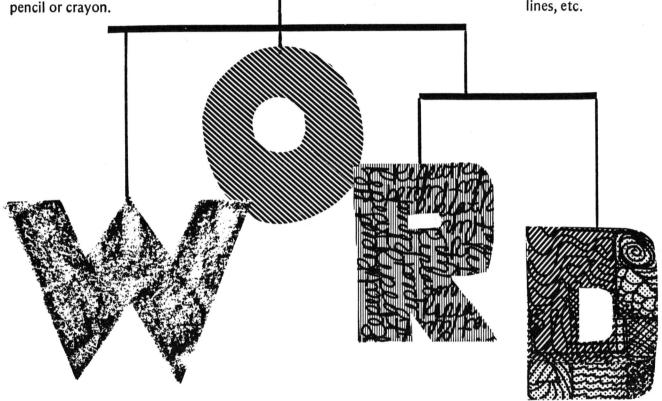

A   WORD   IS   WORTH   A   THOUSAND   PICTURES.

choose

SPLASH

quiet shady street i estored Old Town

mediocrity.

sophisticated

KICKOFF

Defy

See

RACE TRACK.

Illustrated

Compromise

WINNING

Decisions...decisions...

Cam

51

FRAMED FAVORITES

Get everybody (including yourself) started on a personal word frame. Use old frames brought from home or frames you've made. Begin filling them with your VERY FAVORITE WORDS. Do this for several days, then keep the frames for adding words throughout the year. USE THESE as starters for writing assignments:

For example:

Use 6 of your words in a color poem.
Make a poster advertising one of the words for sale.
Write a speech telling what is fantastic about one of the words.
Use three of your framed words in a joke.
Make three of the words into a tongue twister.

Start yours here

. . . and many, many other writing tasks . . . . . .

WORDS ON THE MOVE

Below are some words for NOT standing still. Ask kids to move their bodies to show the meaning of each. (They don't have to <u>know</u> the meanings.)

wiggle	wobble
pirouette	twist
flutter	shiver
fluctuate	swoop
gallop	tremble
amble	strut

Find other words for moving. Talk about the subtle differences between the meanings of the words.

WORD SCAVENGERS

Get kids learning new words by sending them on a scavenger hunt for words right in their own environments. To show that they know what the word means, they must bring an object to school. Look for such items or colors or textures as:

lozenge	vase	tumeric	thesaurus
jute	syringe	chamois	wrench
vise	mallet	coaster	coarse
khaki	woven	abrasive	emerald

5 WORDS TO KEEP

Tell students that you are taking away all the words in the world except 5. Ask them to choose which 5 they would like to keep. Take time for sharing the words and their reasons for keeping them. Later you might ask them to write a phrase next to each word telling what's special about it—thereby building a poem. Here's mine:

Joy — my favorite feeling and my sister
Pumpkin — for pie and jack-o-lanterns
Yes! — for I DO! I agree! I CAN! I will!
Hugging — a good way to love and be loved
You — I don't ever want to be without—YOU!

Graffiti ⟶

A cow eating grass is a lawn mooer.

WEREWOLVES MOONLIGHT!

A baseball! bat is a fly swatter.

WELCOME TO:
Oompa, Pa.
POPULATION 10,796

KAY *were were sure*

$$+ \frac{2's}{8's}$$
tennis

one lips
tulips
3 lips

MT. EVEREST is lazy

53

A FISH that blows BUBBLES is a RAINBOW TROUT

LANGUAGE DELIGHT and CLASSROOM LIFE

During a school week there are literally scores of corners and crannies into which can be woven "poetic experiences"—games and happenings and small influences that act as living examples of the joys in language. I believe that a playful but serious language-loving teacher can be constantly and subtly building vocabularies, stretching imaginations, strengthening usage skills and fertilizing enthusiasm for language. Try to watch for such opportunities during your day. Here are ONE DOZEN of the many, many possibilities (they only take minutes!):

1. When you call roll or take lunch count, do it in poetry·

    Good morning, Tom—I'd like to say
    It's certainly fine to have you back today!

    You look sleepy, Sue—but that's all right—
    I didn't get much sleep either last night.

    OR line up to couplets:

    If you have shoes the color of mine,
    It's your turn to get in line.

2. During a spelling test, instead of:

    The man put oil in his car.

    use sentences such as:

    The slimy oil oozed across the sizzling sidewalk and slithered over the curb.

3. Use those extra standing-in-line or calming-down moments to finish a limerick, brainstorm synonyms, make up couplets, gather lists of rhyming words, play rhyme games with names, etc.

    Who can think of a word that rhymes with my name and means "ornery"?

4. Hang up challengers around the room:

Next to a poem: *Bet you can't learn this by Thursday!*
Beside a graffiti mural of superlatives: *Can you add two?*
Above a HOW MANY WAYS TO SAY 'WIN'? poster: *Sign your name if you've added a synonym for "won."*

5. YOU bring in a WORD I'M CRAZY ABOUT (maybe every day?). Teach it to the kids, then USE it many times throughout the day.

If this noise doesn't <u>abate</u>, I may start screaming!

6. OFTEN—stop and fuss over words and special combinations of words that you come to when reading a story or a passage from a textbook.

"PARABOLA" . . . doesn't that word feel bubbly in your mouth? Try saying it ten times real fast! Tammy, would you get the word book and add that to the page of "Words to Say When Your Mouth is Full"?

7. Trade a word each week with another class. When your class gets its word-for-the-day, make a big deal out of it. Maybe make a rule that each person has to use it during the day or week in at least five different ways. Then do something very special with it (build a painting around it, make it the title for a movie, create an acrostic with it, use it in a poem, etc.). Share the special creation with the other class.

8. Listen to lots of records together. Song lyrics are usually poetry —and often they use words in creative combinations. You might suggest that your students add verses of their own or substitute better words and phrases.

9. YOU memorize and burst into a poem or a riddle or a pun—spontaneously—often! When the day or the period needs livening, that's the time for you to start in:

> *"One fine day, in the middle of the night,*
> *Two dead men got up to fight ...."*

10. Be on the lookout for descriptive or especially pleasing phrases. Ask kids to bring one from home for tomorrow's homework or find one in the reading book, or look for one at the library or cut one from a magazine or make one up. I call this "listening for the velvet":

> *". . . in the fern-deep grove at the midnight end of the garden."*

11. Do lots of poetry together—listen to it, memorize it, share it, march to it, set it to music, chant it, speak it in choirs, have a Poetry Party—and invite others to hear the poems you've learned.

12. Send kids searching for phrases that create pictures in their minds. Then use paint or clay or ink or paper or crayon or another medium to reproduce the images. Display the visual art along with the words. One of my favorite dual image pieces is a gold and green spray painting done by a third grader to match:

> *"a slice of slivered moon in a green sky"*

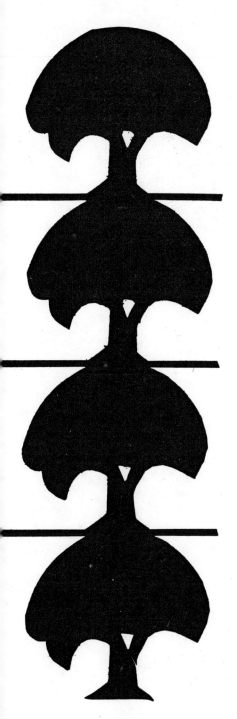

HOW TO ADAPT A GOOD IDEA TO YOUR WRITERS

The ideas of this chapter are suitable to a number of ages and purposes, depending on

. . . the subject or topic you choose

. . . the simplicity or complexity of the words you use

. . . the number of examples required

. . . the duration of the exercise

. . . the extent to which the activity is developed

. . . the extending exercises suggested

. . . the teacher's expectations

. . . the amount of writing involved

WHAT DO YOU KNOW ABOUT A TREE? may be adapted like this:

For non-writers — Each student in the circle gives one idea related to "tree." When everyone has had a turn, continue until the ideas run out. The teacher may write a list, if she wishes to have it for later use.

For young writers — Same as above, only move on to additional topics in small groups. If a list is written on one of the topics, then give an assignment that requires writing one sentence using at least four of the words.

For older writers — Brainstorm words with students in pairs. Try several topics. Ask them to collect the list on one topic (either with the whole group or in their partnerships). Then give another ten minutes for them to create a new list on the same topic that uses none of the other words.

For Jr. High or gifted writers — Same as above—also, fill a blackboard with as many words as possible related to a football game. Then ask them to write a one-paragraph description of a football game WITHOUT USING ANY of the words on the board. This forces the brainstorming process to continue.

Aunt Marge: *"Oh, kids, look at the full moon!"*

Krista, age 3:   *"What's it full of?"*

Scotty, age 2:   *"Does it have a zipper so you can fill it up?"*

"They groan when it's time for writing!"

♥ ROMANCE ♥

3

WHAT'S GOING ON HERE?

This morning some writing sessions are in progress at Lincoln School:

... John Ebel's eighth grade language arts students are building sculptures of wire, wood, styrofoam, foil, clay and other materials to communicate such themes as "awe," "poverty," "rage," "conflict," "pride," "renewal," "contentment."

... Margie Boyle's fourth graders are stroking feathers, blowing them in the air, then catching them on elbows, toes, noses, heads.

... Peggy Nicholson's third graders are eating peanut butter.

... Kids in Angela Giavanni's EMR resource room are talking about how it feels to be afraid.

... Don O'Neill's sixth grade reading group is reading horoscopes.

... Second graders in Jacob Walsh's class are visiting a local cemetery.

... Carol Rawlings' third period seventh grade social studies students are drawing around each other's bodies and painting life-sized portraits.

... Students in Carmen Reid's fifth grade are tasting dishes their families contributed to an international smorgasbord.

... Liz Freeberg's first graders are lying on the floor in the dark listening to a scary song about a "Grebigol."

... Michael Alton's nervous third graders are just lining up for German measles shots.

"Writing sessions?" you're asking yourself. Yes, writing sessions! These kids are being romanced! They're in the midst of an important beginning stage of the writing process; their minds and spirits are being touched by

... the discoveries that entice description

... the sensual experiences that spur verbal images

... the discussions that dredge up memories

... the questions that beg for hypotheses

... the stimuli that release words.

STARTING LOVE AFFAIRS WITH IDEAS

> ### BIAS #9   THE INPUT DETERMINES THE OUTPOUR
>
> *Experiences—with self, with others, with literature, with arts—are the catalysts that ignite expression. The hearing, enjoying, sharing, trying, discussing, remembering, discovering of life and literature NATURALLY flow into writing.*

It's happened so often that I'm tempted to guarantee it for you: when I go into a classroom and get kids involved in a doing or talking experience, or when I start sharing literature with a special appeal—KIDS ASK TO WRITE! Last year I visited a class, prepared to read a cycle of WARNING poems and start them writing some of their own. The teacher cautioned me that the class was rowdy and uncreative, so I was ready with ten exciting motivating poems. After four, their pencils were out and one little boy said, "Would you be quiet so we can write our own?"

PLEASE, don't ask kids to write without giving them some input! It doesn't have to come immediately before the writing (although often it should be fresh). The input can be ongoing exposure to literature or yesterday's science experiment that flopped. But SOMETHING romantic needs to precede the writing assignment: some happening that jars loose the poetry inside their heads and sets free a flow of new ideas.

If you come in (as I did one April afternoon in 1970) with:

> *"Okay, kids . . . today is the first day of spring; isn't it exciting to have the sunshine back after a long winter? Let's all write a poem about spring. You have twenty minutes until recess, so get started quickly."*

probably most of them will write (especially if you threaten "no recess" for those who don't) but you'll get:

> *I like spring*   *(an actual result of the*
> *It makes me sing*   *above assignment)*
> *It is a nice thing*
> *Ding-a-ling.*
>   *The End*

and you won't be happy with it . . . . . . and neither will they!

The next year I tried the romance:

—This time we all moved outside with paper and pencils and one large piece of posterboard.

—For 15 minutes we lay on our backs in silence—breathing the air, tasting the wind, watching and feeling spring.

—We dug our bare feet into the dirt
       rolled in the grass
       picked up bugs
       inspected tender buds.

—Then, we gathered under a tree and made a list of all the sights and sounds and smells and feelings and tastes and sensations of spring.

—With that list as our source of ideas and inspiration, each of us moved slightly away from the others and wrote . . . and wrote. I asked each to do at least two poems. Some kids wrote ten.

Poems such as these appeared, accompanied by proud smiles:

My principal wasn't sure about such outdoor expeditions—especially when neighbors called to ask, "Are you aware there is a teacher rolling down the hill in your school yard—what is going on over there?" So I learned to inform him ahead of time, invite him to join us, and show off our finished work. One year we even delivered to the neighbors a Remember the day you saw us rolling in the grass? Here's what we were doing! *poetry brag bulletin.*

New mown grass smells prickle my nose,
New-born flies whisper in my ears,
Damp new dirt pets my bare feet,
Fresh new air teases my tongue.
A brand new spring brings
          smiles to my heart.
            Amy, Grade 4

Spring comes.
Worms wiggle.
Flies bother.
Bugs chase each other.
Sunshine warms you.
Teachers let kids outside.
Spring comes.
          Jonathan, Grade 4

An ant crawled over my leg
And back on to the grass.
He didn't even care that I was here.
          Tom, Grade 4

WHERE DO WRITERS GET IDEAS?

Meanwhile, back in the classrooms:

... Mr. Ebel's students have finished their sculptures. Now they are sculpting with words: writing poems to match the themes of their artwork.

... The feather-blowing in fourth grade has moved into word collecting. The word collections are offering selections for lines in cinquains:

<table>
<tr><td>Feather</td><td>Feather</td></tr>
<tr><td>Fluffy, silky</td><td>Airy, tickly</td></tr>
<tr><td>Twirling, tumbling, floating</td><td>Blowing, turning, twisting</td></tr>
<tr><td>Soft as melted marshmallow</td><td>Light as an empty eggshell</td></tr>
<tr><td>Feather</td><td>Fluff</td></tr>
</table>

... The peanut butter eaters are writing TV commercial scripts for various kinds of peanut butter.

... In Angela's room, the "afraid" phrases have been gathered and arranged into a collaborative poem:

> *When you're afraid,*
> *Your hands get watery,*
> *You feel cold all over,*
> *And you want to hold something.*
> *Your breathing changes*
> *And your heart bangs in your ears,*
> *And your stomach jumps around.*
> *It's like being inside a black closet.*

... Mr. O'Neill's reading class is writing its own horoscope column for the sixth grade monthly newsletter.

... At the cemetery, second graders are making up original epitaphs.

... Each seventh grader has completed a portrait depicting one of his or her roles in life. They are writing role autobiographies describing the norms of behavior for that role.

... The smorgasbord patrons have generated a list of descriptive phrases for their entrees (for later use in composing menus):

> —soft, shimmery noodles
> —chewy red meat huddled in a smooth rice wrapper
> —crunchy with sweet peppers
> —moistness of tender beef tidbits against a brittle
>   crunch of almonds
> —oily pork morsels
> —a sauce of syrupy maple
> —slender celery fingers oozing with tart yogurt
> —chin-dripping firecracker tomato sauce
> —. . . with a blanket of the sweetest cream

... The song about the Grebigol now has two new verses added by first graders caught in the spooky spirit of mysterious monsters.

... Mr. Alton's third graders, back from getting shots, are telling and writing jokes about needles and doctors.

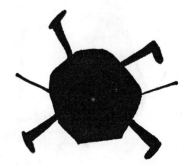

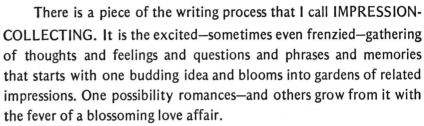

There is a piece of the writing process that I call IMPRESSION-COLLECTING. It is the excited—sometimes even frenzied—gathering of thoughts and feelings and questions and phrases and memories that starts with one budding idea and blooms into gardens of related impressions. One possibility romances—and others grow from it with the fever of a blossoming love affair.

It is this process that supplied the raw material for the writing going on in the ten classrooms we've visited. The same process breeds ideas for most writers I know. Carol, my poet-neighbor, has stacks of cards with jotted-down impressions and possibilities that she's been collecting all summer in preparation for a new book. My husband has notebooks full of observations and half-essays from which he draws writing material. My friend Don, who writes songs, has a briefcase strewn with scraps of paper on which are scribbled lines and thoughts and parts of verses (some are years old) that eventually become lyrics. And <u>this</u> book is being formed today from files of thoughts and ideas and notes—some are recent inspirations; others have been lying dormant in folders for ten years.

Isn't this what writing is? . . . the combining of notions and parts of ideas into precise final works? How can children truly have the experience of such writing, then, unless they have been given the time and incitement to gather the ideas?

I have this notion that ideas are sequestered some place within every body—maybe in heads or hearts or limbs or stomachs—and that a teacher's task is to offer maps so the ideas can travel out through mouths and pencils.

> ### BIAS #10   IT'S HARD TO WRITE IN A VACUUM
> *Writing ISN'T taught by saying, "Write . . . ," then grading what kids already know how to do. Writing IS taught by suggesting challenging directions, presenting patterns and providing examples that open doors to original thinking and expressing.*

Even adults (including those who make their livings as writers) need catalysts—not every time they pick up a pencil, but as continuing forces in their creative lives. So don't be afraid to provide a theme or offer a form or plant an idea. It won't stifle individuality—if you're open enough to allow it to go in any direction or flexible enough to permit total deviation from your idea.

Many sections of this book supply examples of such directions—particularly Chapters 2, 8 and 10. THIS CHAPTER'S PURPOSE is to share with you the HOW of sending kids down those paths.

"Giving an assignment" COULD consist of:

"Write an advertisement for this jar of peanut butter."

That is NOT what I mean by "offering direction." I mean suggesting a possible form and topic for writing by romancing the student with the idea so thoroughly that she is intimate with that jar of peanut butter . . .

   . . . She knows how it tastes and smells.

   . . . She knows how it spreads on fresh bread.

   . . . She's felt it on her fingers and had it stuck to the roof of her mouth.

   . . . She's found out how other people like it.

   . . . She's familiar with its ingredients.

   . . . She's a believer in its value and salability.

   . . . She has a collection of convincing slogans for selling it.

. . . . even before she begins to write that ad.

So . . . the ensuing pages offer you designs for romancing writers . . . by saturating them with the creating, doing, thinking, discussing, sensitizing experiences that give them reasons to get out their pencils.

OPERATION SATURATION . . . . . . WITH LITERATURE

There are many possibilities for using literature as a stimulator:

START WITH A WHOLE BOOK . . . . . .

****

Anybody—of any age—can relate to *Alexander and the Terrible Horrible, No Good, Very Bad Day,* by Judith Viorst, because everybody has had at least one terrible, horrible day! Enjoy the book with your first or tenth graders . . . then share your "bad day" experiences . . . then write . . .

. . . a list of the ten things that happened to you on your very worst day

OR . . . the story of the most horrible day in your life

OR . . . a directory of things to say (or not to say) to a person who is having an awful day

OR . . . a list of ten things that might happen to make a very GOOD day for you .

****

OR . . . START WITH JUST HALF OF A BOOK . . . . . .

Many books (fiction or not) have captivating beginnings and stopping places just right for enticing young writers to carry on the tale.

****

Fortunately by Remy Charlip, is a good news-bad news story about a boy who is invited to a surprise party and encounters all sorts of fortunes and misfortunes as he tries to get there. Each page adds an adventure or misadventure to the tale. Read aloud the first six or eight pages of such a story. Then ask students to finish it orally or in writing. Young children can take turns adding one incident as they orally pass the story around a circle. Older students may write 3 more "fortunately" or "unfortunately" statements to conclude the adventure.

****

OR . . . USE SOME BRIEF SELECTIONS FROM A BOOK . . . . . .

```
* * * * * * * * * * * * * * * * * * * * * * * * * * * * * * * * * * * *
*   Read some cures from Alvin Schwartz' Cross Your Fingers, Spit in      *
*   Your Hat:                                                             *
*                                                                         *
*           If you catch a cold, fry some onions, mix them                *
*           with turpentine, and spread them on your chest.               *
*           . . . or kiss a mule on the nose.                             *
*                                                                         *
*           If freckles cause you to suffer . . . rub ripe                *
*           strawberries or cucumber slices on (them) or                  *
*           cover them for a few minutes each day with                    *
*           mud or cow manure.                                            *
*                                                                         *
*           If you catch the chicken pox, lie on the floor                *
*           of a chicken house and get somebody to chase a                *
*           flock of hens over you.                                       *
*                                                                         *
*   Then make up and laugh at and write some of your own cures for        *
*   hiccups or moles or sore throats or curly hair or no hair or bunions  *
*   or warts or sniffles or varicose veins or . . . . . .                 *
* * * * * * * * * * * * * * * * * * * * * * * * * * * * * * * * * * * * *
```

OR . . . SHARE A POEM TO IMITATE . . . . . .

```
* * * * * * * * * * * * * * * * * * * * * * * * * * * * * * * * * * * *
*   Listen to "Love Song for a Jellyfish" by Sandra Hochman (from         *
*   Earthworks, Viking Press). Then write your own love songs to: your    *
*   nose, old sneakers, a porcupine, a thunderstorm, lightning bugs,      *
*   fog . . . . . .                                                       *
*                      Love Song to My Eraser                             *
*                                                                         *
*           Oh, eraser on my pencil's end                                 *
*           How long you've been my teeth-marked friend!                  *
*           How many times have you been bit?                             *
*           I love you so, I cannot quit!                                 *
*           My teeth chomped in one time too many,                        *
*           Oh, no, my pencil top is empty!                               *
* * * * * * * * * * * * * * * * Vicki, Grade 8  * * * * * * * *
```

69

OR . . . START WITH A CYCLE OF PIECES ON ONE THEME . . . . . .

This can be done with poems or other kinds of literature. It's very effective to use five or six pieces of different kinds on one theme. (For example, try to find a poem, news article, joke, essay, etc. that focus on the same topic.)

****
*   "Warning" and "Early Bird" (Where the Sidewalk Ends by Shel   *
*   Silverstein) along with "If You Should Meet a Crocodile" (from My   *
*   Tang's Tungled, Sara and John Brewton) and several other warning   *
*   poems, motivated students to make a list of all the things they'd   *
*   been warned NOT to do (plus some hypothetical warnings). From   *
*   this list they wrote . . .   *

If you cross your eyes
They'll probably stick.
If you eat with dirty fingernails
You'll end up sick.
                    Jane, Grade 1

If you ever smoke
You will surely choke
If you ever drink
You'll stop being able to think.
If you ever lie
You'll get in trouble and die.
                    Allison, Grade 5

Don't ever put watermelon seeds
In your nose or in your ears
Or you will have a watermelon patch
Covering your head in a few years.

Your skull will turn green
And get stripes like a rind,
And sweet pink juice
Will drip from your mind.

And before you know it—
We know this without a doubt—
You'll end up in a picnic basket
If you don't watch out.
                    Jerry, Steve and Dave, Grade 5

Never tickle an elephant,
For when an elephant starts to
Grin
Cackle
Laugh
And giggle,
An elephant loses her balance
And begins to topple
And you never want to be close
To a falling elephant!
                    Sharon, Grade 3

****

OPERATION SATURATION . . . . . . WITH MUSIC

LISTEN TO WORDLESS MUSIC . . . . . .

. . . and let the melodies and moods and rhythms induce . . .

- . . . word lists
- . . . lines and phrases
- . . . song lyrics
- . . . descriptions of feelings
- . . . word-images
- . . . a letter
- . . . a protest
- . . . a slogan
- . . a poem

(Try music of differing styles and feelings, changing the writing suggestions to match the particular mood of the piece.)

OR . . . LISTEN TO SONGS . . . . . .

. . . then   . . . change words
- . . . add a verse
- . . . invent titles
- . . . design record covers
- . . . write something that follows the theme of the song

* *

After listening to Carole King's *"You've Got A Friend"* (from her *Tapestry* album) write . . .

- . . . a word portrait of an ideal friend for you
- OR . . . an essay on friendship
- OR . . . a tribute to your best friend
- OR . . . a list of ten friendly things to do

* *

OPERATION SATURATION . . . WITH SELVES . . . . . .

Everybody has a ME, and knows some things about his or her SELF—so the topic is an immediate motivator for all ages.

* *

Gather up some pocket mirrors, and ask kids to bring old snapshots of themselves from home. Once everyone has a mirror and a picture, start comparing today's selves to "old" selves by asking kids to think about their then-and-now physical appearance, favorite things to do, hobbies, beliefs, fears, preferences, friends, etc. Then write, following this form:

I used to be _____

But now I am _____

I used to be _____

But now I am _____

I USED TO BE

I used to be chubby
But now I'm thin.

I used to be messy
But now I'm neat.

I used to hate boys
But now I only hate them a little.

I used to be clumsy
But now I'm coordinated.

I used to be afraid of big kids
But now I'm a big kid.

I used to be nine
But now I'm ten.

Janice, Grade 5

* *

There are more ME ideas in Chapter 8.

OPERATION SATURATION . . . WITH ART . . . . . .

The visual arts stimulate "painting with words" and writing leads easily into creating with color and form. Since the two flow so naturally together, try mixing them often in your classroom!

Some DIP 'N DYE sessions with food coloring and squares of paper toweling yielded yards of brilliant banners and room dividers and flags and wrapping paper . . . AND a lot of excitement about color! That excitement led to the associating of colors with feelings, tastes, sounds, smells, thoughts, sights and experiences:

GREEN

The taste of a pickle
The sound of crickets chirping—these are green.

Spring and mint and freshly mown grass smell green.
Green is mold.

Green is the color of pride.
Green is sour.
Green is a tree, rushing water, and a slimy frog.

Green is a flouride treatment at the dentist.
Green is the feeling you get when your best friend moves.
And green is spinach and broccoli
And the way a sourball pinches your tongue.

Green is crunchy.

A collaboration by fifth graders

BROWN IS . . .

Brown is a brownie and a fox
Brown is a chocolate milkshake.
Boxes are brown,
And brown is some rootbeer.
Brown is the feeling you have on a winter day.

It's mud, it's a turkey
A cow, cocoa wheats and a fall day.
Brown is a beagle and a dirty pig.
Sometimes my baby sister's bottom is brown.

Brown is gingerbread baking
Homework is brown.
Brown is getting in fights with your friends
And eating something you don't like.

Brown is being hungry,
Getting punished is brown.
Brown is failing in school
Or having your foot fall asleep.

A collaboration by second graders

73

OPERATION SATURATION . . . WITH MOVEMENT . . . . . .

The act of moving the body awakens creative thinking and rouses the words that help interpret feelings.

If you're going to write about a lion, spend time

MOVING like a lion . . sleeping or waking or yawning
  . . . stalking its prey
  . . . prowling through grasslands
  . . . playing with cubs
  . . . devouring dinner
  . . . caged in a zoo

. . . THEN write . . . some LION-sized words
  OR . . . lion lies
  OR . . . lion conversations
  OR . . . lion tales

Try moving like various animals or natural forces, etc. and at the same time, create movement phrases:

"a swirling, howling wind"
"flounder and flail like a fish on dry land"
"oozing, melting butter"
"a proud stalking lion"
"water gushing and plummeting over a waterfall"
"a slouching, slinking black cat"
"a strutting peacock"
"meandering along like a lazy river"
"chipmunks all a-scurry"

Use bodies to explore and dance different feelings . . . then compose I CAN DANCE poems:

I can dance JOY . . .
I can dance HURT . . .
I can dance EMBARRASSMENT . . .
I can dance ANGER
And BOREDOM . . .
I can dance SURPRISE . . .
I can dance LOVE . . .
I can dance RAGE.
  Collaboration by second and third graders

Perform the dances with the poem.

OPERATION SATURATION . . . WITH GROUP ADVENTURES . . .

A thunderstorm that passes your window . . . a bumblebee that enters your window . . . a walk around the block . . . a popcorn party . . . a game you lost in gym . . . all are provokers of thoughts and feelings fit for writing.

* *

A group unpacking of a grocery bag filled with fruits and vegetables, followed by some touching and tasting of the foods, resulted in word lists, riddles, poems, tributes, essays and other written works by a multi-aged group of kids and adults:

Who Am I?

I'm scrumptious
And tender and juicy—
Delicious with cream or alone,
My skin is as soft as velvet
But my heart is hard as stone.

10 Reasons to Ban Watermelon

1. *It's sloppy.*
2. *It's noisy to eat.*
3. *It messes up the refrigerator.*
4. *It mushes up the fruit salad.*
5. *It gets stains on your clothes.*
6. *The seeds stop up the garbage disposal.*
7. *It crowds the garbage.*
8. *It breaks the bag on the way home from the supermarket.*
9. *You have to buy more than you want.*
10. *You always have to throw out a lot and children are starving in Africa.*

IT'S THE PITS!

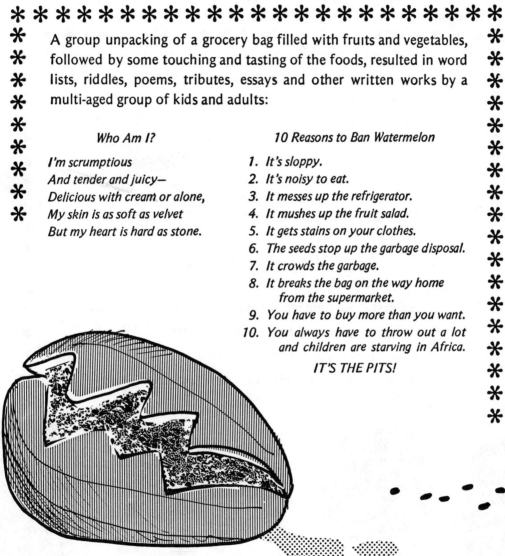

OPERATION SATURATION ... WITH ... JUST TALKING ......

You know how special are those times when someone starts to tell a personal anecdote, and immediately others chime in with, "Oh, ya— — I've had that happen too!" Some very rewarding writing experiences emerge from shared memories and common feelings.

```
* * * * * * * * * * * * * * * * * * * * * *
*   My students loved to hear me tell about              *
*      ...the time I had to stand in the wastebasket in an eighth grade   *
*          social studies class for talking during a test.               *
*      ...the spanking I got for serving water from the toilet to my least  *
*          favorite aunt.                                                 *
*      ...the day I gave a speech to 200 people—with my zipper open.      *
*                                                                         *
*                                                                         *
*   After you've told some, ask students to share their memories in small  *
*   groups, then to write about                                          *
*      ...the most embarrassing situation of my life                     *
       ...the worst trouble I've ever been in                            *
       ...the stupidest thing I did when I was little                    *
       ...something that happened to me in kindergarten                  *
       ...something I'm really glad happened to me                       *
```

...my first violin lesson (or bike ride or kiss or spanking or recital or valentine)

OPERATION SATURATION ... WITH ... A FEELING YOU CAN'T IGNORE ......

Some of the best writing situations arise spontaneously out of a need to articulate a feeling that's rampant in the classroom. It may be a feeling of   ... excitement over an accomplishment
... anticipation of a special occasion
... anxiety about an upcoming challenge
... hurt or disappointment about a change in plans
... anger resulting from mistreatment

Writing about those feelings often helps them to be dissipated or savored or re-directed. _____

* *

Once my class returned from music with hostility running high over alleged insults from their music teacher. We started talking about "what really makes me mad" and gradually the complaints moved away from the individual to general irritating situations in the world. Soon we were laughing together instead of gnashing teeth! I asked the students to make personal "Don't You Just Hate_____?" lists. Here's one started by a teacher. Add two of your own to the list:

Don't you just hate *when you get a new student—and nobody bothered to* *inform you ahead of time?* _____

Don't you just hate *when the principal comes to observe just at the moment that* *Bob is biting Julie's leg?* _____

Don't you just hate *when the fire bell rings just after you've gotten every-* *body quieted down and started on their work?* _____

Don't you just hate _____

Don't you just hate _____

* *

OPERATION SATURATION . . . WITH CONTENT AREA EXPERIENCES . . . . . .

Watch for those times when imagination and writing skills can grow out of a lesson, unit or activity in other subject areas.

✳ ✳

One fourth grade science class, studying a unit on weather, concluded each experiment by concocting a news article, complete with smashing headline, to capsulize the results of the experiment. (Some of their articles were serious, others genuinely frivolous.)

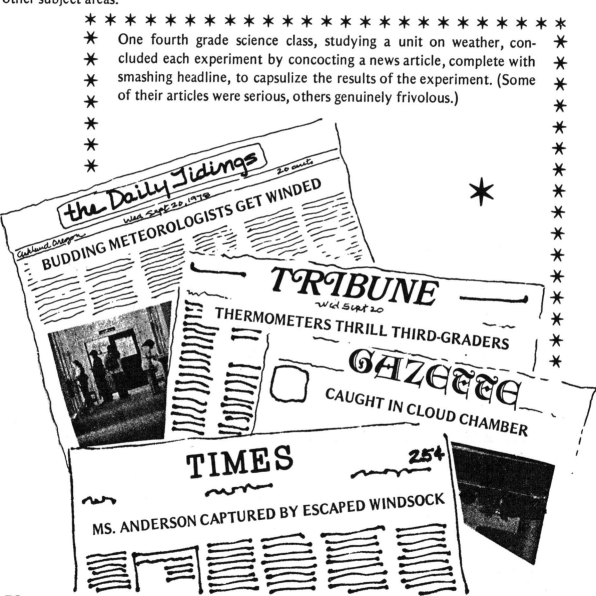

WHICH MOTIVATORS ARE RIGHT FOR YOU?

> ### BIAS #11   THERE IS NO ONE WAY
> There isn't any ONE never-fail recipe for getting kids to write or appreciate writing. A good motivator is something that WORKS—for YOU and your students.

Some advice for you to consider as you choose stimulators from this book or other sources:

1. INCLUDE A VARIETY OF STARTERS DURING THE YEAR. Not all kids prefer the same selections or have the same needs or turn on to the same assignments. Gather for yourself enough options to appeal to every kid. The more directions you try, and the more divergent your offerings, the better are your chances for reaching every writer.

2. LISTEN TO YOUR KIDS. Watch what they like, what they relate to, what they CAN do. Listen to them in the cafeteria and on the playground. Pay attention to their wishes and dreams and plans and schemes. Use the stuff that's IN them . . . and draw upon the things they KNOW for stimulation.

3. LISTEN TO YOURSELF. YOU are an individual too. Not all teachers prefer the same activities; different things work for different people. You may bring out a bowl of fruit as a writing starter and find your kids think you're nuts! Then you'll wonder . . . "What on earth was Marge Frank thinking when she wrote THIS idea?" What works for me may not be comfortable for you, so start with some of the ideas that excite you, first. Then gradually toy with new ones. If one is a flop, don't feel like a rotten teacher! There are hundreds of others!

4. SOMETIMES, USE <u>NO</u> MOTIVATORS. Every group of kids needs chances to JUST write. And on those occasions, don't worry about the lack of stimulus because, if you're filling kids up with experiences and literature regularly, THAT INPUT ACCUMULATES and becomes a source of creative thinking for all future writing.

5. FOR MORE AID, see Chapter 8's special sections on ideas for particular kinds of writers AND Chapter 7's suggestions for working with reluctant writers and young writers AND Chapter 10's starters for independent writers.

Kids can overdose on too many motivators! It isn't necessary to start with a new stimulator daily. Yes, they need a variety of writing experiences, but they should also have a chance to stay with one form or idea long enough to develop it thoroughly. And sometimes it's valuable to return to a form several times—each time developing more sophistication.

Let the topic determine the form! Memories are shared well through diaries or flash-back stories, while discussion of the future leads naturally into writing predictions or horoscopes and fortunes.

PROCESS

"But teaching writing is such hard work!"

HERE I AM IN THE MIDDLE OF A BOOK.. ....

Right! Teaching writing IS hard work! WRITING is hard work! The past two months of my life prove that. How many times this summer I have wished that you and your students could be watching over my shoulder—because so much of what I'm trying to say about the writing process is happening to me right now!

I came to this project with a myriad of writing-related experiences. My family filled my early years with literary appreciation and I've given long hours to written assignments as a high school student and an English major in college. For ten years I've tried countless writing ideas with my own elementary and college students. In a recent summer I spent three months in virtual non-stop preparation for a series of writing seminars with teachers. I've read miles of pages on the subject, taken copious notes, pawed through children's books and poetry anthologies and stacks of kids' writing I've saved. Again and again I've sorted through my beliefs, visited dozens of classrooms to write with kids of all ages, presented workshops and talked with hundreds of teachers in cities all over the country. AND . . . I've written other books . . . and articles . . and speeches. So I ought to have been ready for this one!

AND YET—in order to write this book—and in spite of my three bulging file boxes labeled, "Stuff for Use in Writing Book," I've still traipsed home from bookstores loaded with new books and holed up for days in libraries, read reams of articles, added folders full of new impressions to my files, tried out scores of thoughts on teacher-friends and worn ragged the pages of my word-finder, thesaurus and grammar guides. The basic outline has been re-worked nine times (each was the last, I was sure) and continues to alter as I begin each chapter. Every time I've met with Judy, the artist, to talk form and concept, I've come home to make a raft of changes. I've written and re-written and thrown away and started over, re-arranged chapters, deleted and added and adapted. (And I'm only on Chapter 4!)

There is struggle and sweat and groaning and restlessness. Sometimes every word is agony. But there is also grinning and pleasure and excitement. When everything is RIGHT— and sentences are flowing spontaneously—the exhilaration can hardly be contained. One night I was so intoxicated by the fervor that I had to stop writing about writing so I could capture in words the intensity of my feelings.

Our students should be told about the energy that writing takes! We need to share with them the WHOLE picture—through all the romantic and unromantic phases: the time, the work, the joy, the pain, the fulfillment. Let's not ever deceive them into thinking that anybody is consistently able to sit down and command beautifully-stated, carefully-organized thoughts to drip off the end of a pencil!

WRITING IS A PROCESS

The cute ideas are not enough.
Diagramming sentences and perfecting possessives won't do it either!
It's more than turn-on or isolated grammatical skills!

Writing is a thinking process, a vital tool for students' lives. If they are to use this tool with dexterity, they need to encounter an approach to the whole writing process that can become their own, one which they can learn and use for life.

That's why this chapter presents a plan for guiding them from beginning blunderings to polishes pieces—a plan that, once learned, is forever theirs. The nine steps that follow comprise an approach for you and your students built upon my observations of the way writing happens. I have taken the process apart for examination because, when teaching writing, it is helpful to make each stage conscious. However, for all writers there are times when it all melts together to become a natural flow and there is little awareness of a separation between the parts.

Before you try the plan, take note of the IFs, ANDs and BUTs which follow it. They are cautions and further explanations about the use of the plan that are as important to its working as are the nine steps.

BIAS #12   NOTHING REPLACES WRITING TOGETHER!

Because it eases the pain, helps kids grow and benefit from one another's thinking, allows them to SEE the process at work and keeps morale high—it is well worth the time it takes to work through the process together (not ALL the time, but OFTEN).

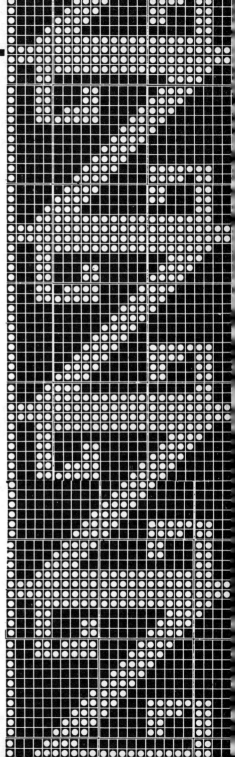

A 9-STAGE PLAN THAT WORKS

STAGE 1   THE MOTIVATION

. . . an experience, a book, an unexpected question, a common feeling . . . You provide the situation or make use of a natural one to evoke ideas, emotions, opinions—to bring to the surface those imaginings which are tucked away in minds.

Notes: *   *Suggest a direction but be loose enough to allow others!*

       *   *Choose high-interest directions—the ones that fascinate kids and the ones that are important for life.*

       *   *See Chapter 3 for more specifics on motivating writing.*

       *   *See Chapter 8 for a bevy of motivators.*

STAGE 2   IMPRESSION-COLLECTING

. . . the gathering of words and fragments and thoughts and facts and questions and observations . . . the process of brainstorming about and broadening of the original idea . . .

Notes: *   *The majority of us need this stage the most. It is crucial to the growth of creative thinking! As teachers, we sometimes cut this short. We're anxious to move on to finished products, so we quit collecting too soon. Allow plenty of time in your classroom for impression-collecting.*

       *   *Fill notebooks and folders with collections. Students can use later what they don't use in to-day's writing.*

       *   *When collecting impressions with and from kids, take EVERYTHING! Let them, rather than you, do the sorting, choosing and censoring.*

       *   *YOU contribute your impressions too! Your additions will encourage divergence, teach new words, show kids how to elaborate on existing ideas, and share your self!*

STAGE 3   THE ROUGH DRAFT

. . . the write-down-your-ideas-as-fast-as-you-can phase . . . This is the stage at which you say, "Okay, you've got thoughts and feelings and impressions, now . . . write! Start putting those pieces together into lines and sentences."

A classroom full of rough draft writers looks like this: people are writing, thinking, mumbling, stopping to swap or share, writing again, calling for help. It's delightfully chaotic! You're there to light the fire and keep it fueled. The kids add the sizzle and crackle.

Note: *   *Do you remember the last time YOU faced a blank page?—maybe you had to write a reference for a colleague, or a thank you note for a gift you couldn't stand or your professional goals for a teaching application. PANIC—right? Recently I set out to write a letter of sympathy to a friend. All my years of grammar lessons and book writing didn't spare me from the terror of that empty white space. I struggled and paced for two hours before the right words came. Remember that pain when you ask kids to write. And help to ease it by:*

    . . . letting them write without stopping to correct . . . You can always go back and fix errors. You can't always recover a lost idea!

    . . . struggling through it together many times . . . This will give them the practice and pattern for doing it alone.

    . . . allowing and encouraging talking and sharing . . . The communication that arises in this stage generates more ideas. The humming, somewhat noisy spirit has a momentum all its own that often sweeps along even the most reluctant writers—and that isn't as likely to happen in total silence.

STAGE 4   RE-READING FOR SENSE AND READABILITY

. . . the skimming-over of a piece to get it out into the light and see how it sounds . . . Now's the time for writers to ask themselves, "Does it make sense?" "Does it say what I intended?" "Do I like it?" "Is it smooth and clear?"

Notes: *   *This reading is intended strictly for the writer. It may be shared with another, but its purpose is the response of the writer to his own work.*

    *   Reading ALOUD is the best editor—because you hear your own choppy lines, mixed up sentences, dull words, over-used expressions. Kids can read to a tape-recorder or to a wall—but try to provide them some means of reading aloud.*

STAGE 5   SHARING FOR RESPONSE

. . . a time for trading papers, or reading to a small group, or showing to the teacher—for the purpose of getting others' reactions, advice, suggestions, affirmation of the strengths and ideas for changes. I call this stage RESPONSE instead of CRITICISM, because it sounds less threatening.

Notes: * *Students may need to be TOLD and SHOWN that criticism includes positive response and is meant to be constructive, not degrading.*

        * *I ALWAYS tell kids, "YOU have the final say. You listen to others' opinions and make use of those recommendations that you believe will improve your writing. When you edit, you don't have to accept or use all the suggestions—including mine."*

        * *Chapter 5 provides more details on teaching kids to be good editors and critics.*

STAGE 6   EDITING

. . . the changing stage . . . including anything from reshuffling words to reworking whole pieces. After the writer has listened to her own words and gained the responses of others, then she's ready to make revisions.

Notes: * *Confine the reworking to one or two areas at a time. Often, when kids try to make everything perfect at once, efforts become dispersed so much that nothing is improved significantly. Especially with beginners, the revising is most effective when it concentrates on a few techniques.*

        * *Teach kids to do the editing—don't do it yourself! Even very young children can do some editing!*

        * *Chapter 5 suggests ways to help kids of all ages learn to rework their own writing.*

STAGE 7 — THE MECHANICS CHECK

. . . the time for inspecting the original draft for spelling, grammar, mechanical, and structural errors and weaknesses . . . This may be the stage at which the teacher takes papers home to note (with something other than a red pencil, please) such problems OR looks over shoulders to point them out. A good deal of this can also be done in student groups.

Note: * *See Chapter 5 for more details on this topic, and for information on how to get kids to do this well by themselves.*

STAGE 8 — THE FINAL COPY

. . . the preparation—using the input of all one's own and others' responses on content and mechanics—of the precise draft . . . followed by the satisfaction and surprise that comes with the finishing of a product . . .

Notes: * *Stages 5-7 may be repeated several times before the writer chooses to begin the final copy.*

* *Talk with kids about the plague of creators: that it-could-always-be-better feeling which often accompanies the finishing of a work. Remind them that there comes a time (for anyone) to quit re-working and be satisfied with the product—at least for the time being.*

STAGE 9 — THE PRESENTING

. . . the showing off or sharing part . . . the use of one's words for communicating to other persons . . . In some way, every finished piece should be made public, if the author chooses!

Notes: * *There are dozens of ways to flaunt writing. Chapter 6 suggests some reasons for sharing— along with a few dozen ideas for doing it. Read those ideas, then add your own!*

* *At the end of this chapter, you'll find a sample lesson that has been broken into the nine steps. That section will show you just how one teacher guided a group of students through the whole process.*

IFs, ANDs and BUTs . . . (Cautions About the Plan)

. . . THE PROCESS IS MORE IMPORTANT THAN THE PRODUCT.

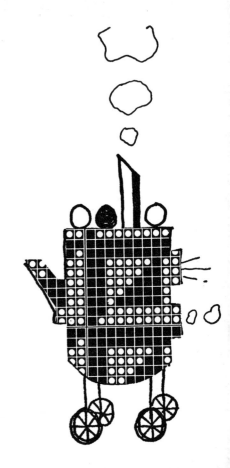

* Accentuate the process. Be vocal about the fact that this is the way writers work and honest about those unromantic phases. Build a bulletin board display around the drafts, showing the changes and the progress. Encourage them to share their drafts with one another.

* Share your own drafts with your students. Let them watch YOUR writing in process. Tell them about the parts that came easily and point out the paragraphs over which you labored. Explain the revisions you made and share your corrections.

* Remember that the real purpose of the plan is to help kids internalize the process. It will become natural for them more quickly if you talk with them every step of the way so that they are aware of what it is they're doing.

* Let parents in on the process, too. Instead of sending home only final products, share ALL the steps and drafts. Have kids add an inscription to the first draft. "Draft #1. Coming soon—Final Draft!"

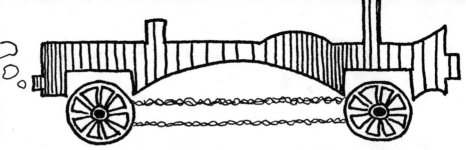

... DON'T ALWAYS GO THROUGH ALL NINE STAGES! !

* If you do a complete autopsy on every piece, your writers may perish from too much pruning. At the least, they'll get weary! REMEMBER THAT EACH STEP OF THE PROCESS IS VALUABLE. If you quit after Stage 2 or 4 or 6, the kids will still have had a significant writing experience.

* But, DO go through all the stages some of the time. If they are never asked to refine or perfect a poem or paragraph, students will quickly get the message that precision and clarity are not important.

... DON'T SKIP THE ROMANCE!

* Avoid starting with Stage 3. I've been guilty of doing that often enough to remember how it leaves students staring at blank pages harboring "I CAN'T" feelings—and to know that the cold plunge into the "Write" stage usually produces awkward, water-logged products.

* Keep alert to the mood of the group. If an assignment is dying . . . bury it! If everybody's captivated by the crow on the windowsill . . . stop everything to watch and write about the crow! If you adapt the writing schedule and the forms to the interests of your writers, they'll be much more ready for Stage 3.

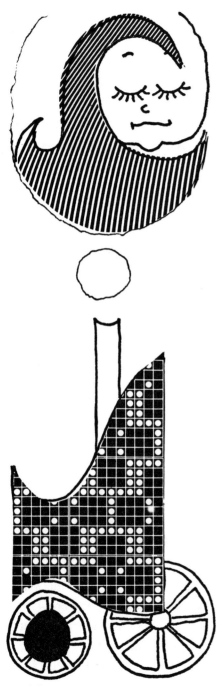

WHAT THE TEACHER DOES WHILE THE KIDS WRITE

You are there to:

1. Inspire and jog ideas from their lodging places, and to keep the assignment alive and fresh.

2. Show them how to collect impressions:

    "Cindy . . . close your eyes . . . you're looking right into that wave . . it's coming toward you . . . what is the water doing? . . . what do you see in the wave? . . . how does it look? . . . sound? . . ."

3. Help them find a form to fit the topic:

    "You've collected a lot of memories you want to share about your dad. Could you maybe bring in some snapshots of him and combine your words with the pictures to make a photo essay?"

    "Jane, it sounds as if you're worried because your family hasn't sold the house yet. How about writing a real estate listing describing all the assets of your home?"

4. Listen and probe and suggest.

5. Ask open-ended questions:

    "What sounds would you hear in a haunted house?"
    "How cold was it on the ice rink?"
    "What thoughts did the boy have while he was lost?"
    "What happened to make it an awful trip?"
    "How does it feel to be the youngest person in a large group?"
    "Who else was around?"

6. Read, admire, chat, encourage. Praise genuinely and specifically:

    "Gregg, that sentence just makes my stomach feel like it's on a roller coaster!'"

    "Barbie . . . 'liquid sky' is a beautiful phrase!"

7. Watch for those who need help. Give them more ideas, combine them with other writers or ask them to write with you.

8. Support their re-writing attempts:

   "That was a wise change!"
   "'Frantic' says so much more than 'worried'."
   "It was a good idea to combine those two sentences . . . it's much smoother now."

9. WRITE yourself! When you do, it transforms the atmosphere because it speaks so loudly for the importance and fulfillment of writing.

"THAT ALL TAKES SO MUCH TIME," YOU'RE SAYING *!*

YES, BUT . . . How much time do you give DAILY to reading and arithmetic? Isn't writing as important a life skill?

ALSO . . . . . . If you're frustrated because it takes so many days to write and re-write and edit and share stories or long essays—try short forms! A class can collect and tell jokes, brainstorm ideas for jokes or make up hilarious situations, split into pairs and write some, read them to partners, gather in small groups for editing and checking mechanics, re-write them and post in a GIG-GLE GALLERY—all in 45 minutes!

BESIDES . . . . Writing is a process . . . so it needn't always start and finish in one lesson. Spread an experience over a few days. Come back to a form later . . build and refine.

AND, ANYWAY . . . Writing is ALWAYS a wise use of time . . . because they're not just learning to write. They're reinforcing reading, speaking and other language skills. AND they're developing the higher-level thinking skills. AND they're sharing themselves with other human beings!

PAINTED POEMS .... A SAMPLE LESSON THROUGH ALL THE STAGES

(A lesson involving a collaboration by a class of fourth graders—but an idea which works nicely for all ages of kids and grown-ups.)

STAGE 1
MOTIVATION

10 minutes

The teacher showed a poem and some sentences in which words were placed on the paper in a way so as to suggest or look like the subject of the poem:

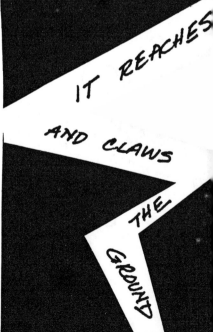

LIGHTNING
SCRATCHES THE SKY
WITH FORKED FINGERS
IT REACHES
AND CLAWS
THE
GROUND

And students talked about other subjects that would work as painted poems or sentences:

rain	a bouncing ball	pole vaulting
a pretzel	tennis	lightening
a tornado	a sandwich	a peacock
walking on stilts	mountain climbing	an ice cream cone
fire	feet	climbing stairs
a rainbow	a sunset	a tornado
a trampolinist	a roller coaster	an octopus
parachuting	a slithering snake	a snail
a home run	a long nose	a pesty fly
a ghost	an earthquake	a tree
a falling leaf	a giraffe	an eraser
		waves

DOWN

STAGE 2
COLLECTING
IMPRESSIONS

8 minutes

The group chose "fireworks" as a theme for a collaborative effort. The teacher asked, "What kinds of things do you see and hear and feel happening when you watch fireworks? Let's make a list of action words."

Students brainstormed LIST 1.

The teacher asked, "What colors do you see when you watch fireworks?" Students collected LIST 2 with the aid of their color word list from the class word book and a thesaurus.

The teacher said, "Pretend that you are seeing fireworks for the first time—and you have NO idea what is causing them. What might be happening to make all those colors in the sky?" Students suggested ideas for LIST 3.

Teacher added "fuscia" and taught students the words "tentacles," "fragments" and "particles."

LIST 1

burn	sprinkle
shoot	drip
explode	light up
crack	fling
hurry	pop
burst	split
spray	crack
streak	crash
splatter	thunder
shatter	opening
sparkle	unfolding

LIST 2

gold	florescent
purple	kaleidoscope
silver	green
red	emerald
crimson	fuscia
violet	hues
turquoise	azure
orange	bright
orchid	brilliant
black sky	
chartreuse	

LIST 3

painting the sky	clouds are exploding
rainbow at night	dropping colors on the trees
throwing out colors	spraying colored water
raining fire	bright confetti in the air
colored octopus arms	particles (fragments) flying
(tentacles)	someone making colored designs
jets making streaks	and patterns in the sky
colored popcorn	turning on lights in the sky
a surprise party	a paintbox bursting open
colored fan	
the world is lighting up	

STAGE 3
ROUGH DRAFT

10 minutes

Students combined words and ideas from the three lists into lines—with the help of teacher-questions such as:

"Which color fits with 'streak'?"
"What should we put with 'splatter'?"
"Which action word goes well with the fan idea?"

The following list was created:

Drip orchid over the trees.
Turn on lights in the sky.
Paint the space with brilliant colors.
Streak gold across the black sky.
Rain azure drops of fire.
Shoot forth crimson tentacles.
Open up a purple fan.
Sprinkle florescent popcorn.
Spray the night with emerald.
Explode orange into the clouds.
Burst open a turquoise surprise.
Fling fuscia fragments.
Splatter the dark with hues.
Light up the world with chartreuse.
Crack and pop and split the night.
Shatter the grey night.

> *In this stage, the creation of lines is purely arbitrary. Take whatever students give—they can be amended later. Do this quickly. You can't take time to vote on each suggested line. Explain to students that, when writing together, everyone may not be completely satisfied with each line—as one would be with one's own writing.*

STAGE 4
RE-READING

1 minute

Two volunteers read alternate lines aloud slowly.

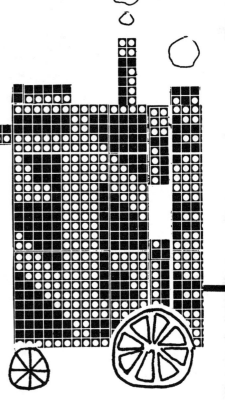
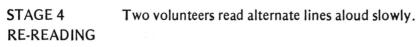

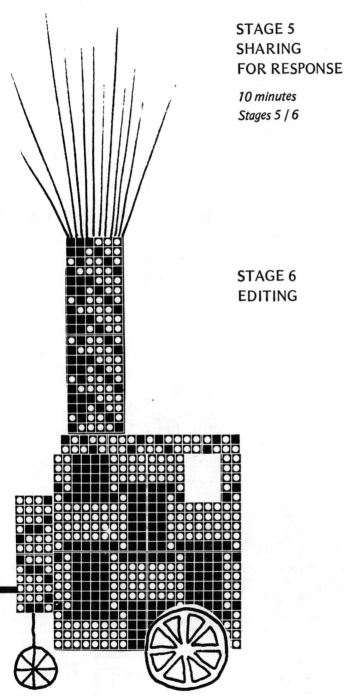

STAGE 5
SHARING
FOR RESPONSE

10 minutes
Stages 5 / 6

The teacher made such inquiries as,
"Which lines do you like just the way they are?"
"Are there any lines too much alike?"
"Do you see any that could be more interesting?"
"Should any lines be dropped?"
"What line would be good for the beginning?"
"What should come next?"
"How shall we end it?"
"What would be a good title?"

The group responded with comments, feelings, additions, while a student stood at the board to note the changes.

STAGE 6
EDITING

The responses from Stage 5 resulted in a general consensus to make the following revisions:

1 *Firecracker, firecracker*
2 *Hurry to the end of your fuse*
   and

7 Drip orchid over the trees.

~~Turn on lights in the sky.~~
   universe
3 Paint the ~~space~~ with brilliant colors.
   ies
5 Streak gold across the black sk~~y~~.

8 Rain azure drops of fire.

9 Shoot forth crimson tentacles.
   unfold *shimmering*
11 ~~Open up~~ a purple fan.

12 Sprinkle florescent popcorn. *in pretty patterns*
   summer
4 Spray the ~~night~~ with emerald.

14 Explode orange into the clouds.

10 Burst open a turquoise surprise.

13 Fling fuscia fragments.

   ~~Splatter the dark with hues.~~
   heavens
6 Light up the ~~world~~ with chartreuse.
   silence
15 Crack and pop and split the ~~night~~.

16 Shatter the grey night.

STAGE 7
MECHANICS-
CHECK
10 minutes

Everyone re-read to search for spelling or structural errors. Some students consulted dictionaries. Together the group decided how to punctuate each line.

STAGE 8
FINAL COPY
20 minutes

Two students agreed to work at copying the revised poem onto a large sheet of paper in the form of fireworks.

STAGE 9
PRESENTING

Another two students added bright-colored chalk lines and designs to strengthen visually the "fireworks" image. On another day, individuals wrote and designed other painted writings. Then all were displayed in the school foyer. Above the display students hung a huge paintbrush and palette (filled with words rather than colors) and a sign saying, "Writers Paint With Words."

 *Whole group time = 50 minutes.*

* *Note: With painted writings, I never hint at the idea of adding color until the words are written in the shape of the topic, or students tend to draw a picture first and "smush" the words into the illustration. The final product is more effective, as is the process, if the words play the central role in creating the form.*

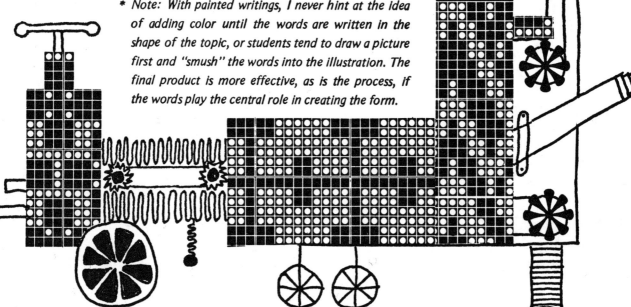

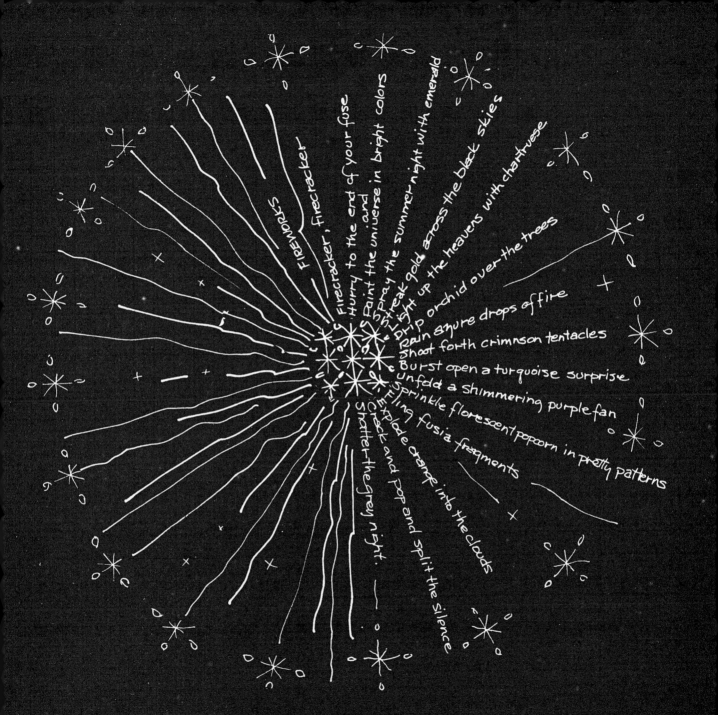

THE SOLDIER

A poem written suddenly
        Outpouring onto paper
Scribbled down hurriedly
        While thoughts are hot still
Becomes a soldier, defiant, free,
        To fight my war, to fight for me.

An onslaught of words, defending me,
        Goes forth like a brave trooper
From his home. And now,
        Without author, stands alone.

But it returns, beaten, red marks like wounds
Slashing the innocent lines,
        The struggle over.
The wounds are deep. They reach
        To scar my soul which cries out:
"Understand!" The feeling, not the grammar,
        Should be read! Now the soldier is dead.
The poem that he was lies crumpled
        In a corner, the effort made in vain.

The enemy has won.

                    by Rencie Farwell
                    Grade 6

TOOLS

"Should spelling and grammar count? How much?"

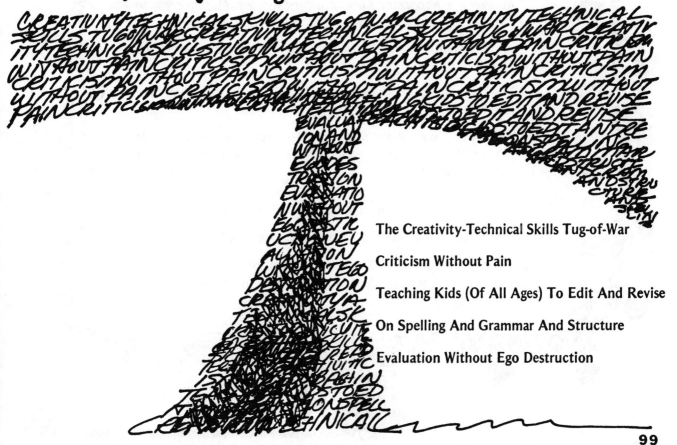

The Creativity-Technical Skills Tug-of-War

Criticism Without Pain

Teaching Kids (Of All Ages) To Edit And Revise

On Spelling And Grammar And Structure

Evaluation Without Ego Destruction

THE CREATIVITY-TECHNICAL SKILLS TUG-OF-WAR

At a dinner party I recently attended, talk turned to the topic of writing:

"Why aren't schools teaching kids to write anymore?"

"Well, my kids write all the time. Their stories are great—but the spelling and grammar are atrocious!"

"What ever happened to basic skills?"

"I'd rather see kids just write. Correcting errors all the time stifles imagination."

"Accuracy is important for expository writing. During creative writing kids should be allowed to write anything—any way."

"All this creativity stuff is a cop-out. Teachers today are just too lazy to teach real writing skills."

"No—the real skill is thinking, and that's more important than spelling!"

"Well I don't care about imagination—I want my kid to be able to write decent sentences. Otherwise he'll never make it through college."

And, "Where," I thought as my dander rose, "is the voice for BOTH?"

And, "Since when," I wondered, "is thinking not a basic?"

And, "Why," I fumed—silently at first, then aloud, "do so many people see ALL-BASICS and NO-BASICS as the only choices?"

> ## BIAS #13   THERE IS NO RIVALRY BETWEEN SKILLS AND CREATIVITY
>
> *Good writing is based on a healthy friendship between imagination and technique. It can and must be taught without slighting either.*

The rivalry exists only in the minds of people who haven't thought much about the true nature of the writing process. Good teachers have always known that freedom to wonder and experiment is crucial for learning to write. They've also known that, for any writer, there comes a time when he must set his bottom on a chair, pick up the pen and write to perfect his message. They know about the marriage of inspiration and discipline in good writing.

All writing is original. Anytime a student writes a question, an explanation, an analysis, she's creating—as surely as if she were inventing a myth. And then—even the most inventive writing has to cope with sequencing of sentences, precise word choice, paragraph organization and placement of punctuation.

I cannot promote dealing with language skills ONLY as they happen to arise during writing. I'll lobby any day for separate, well-planned activities concentrating on those skills. But, I believe we're being dishonest with students if we teach skills in the morning language arts period and then, during afternoon creative writing, say, "Never mind that stuff." The writing setting is too fine an opportunity for strengthening and making relevant those tools to be leaving them out. And including work on them does not have to interfere with anybody's originality! This chapter is about how to combine the two.

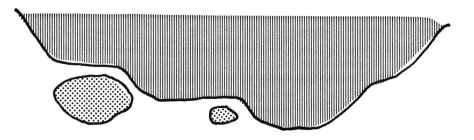

CRITICISM WITHOUT PAIN

CRITICISM: the art of considering merits and demerits and judging accordingly

I mentioned early my lack of excitement about the word "criticize" because of its association with fault-finding—which is of little value to the task of teaching kids to write. I much prefer the idea of "response," and suggest that, if "criticism" is used, students understand that it includes identification of strengths in original drafts—to bolster self-confidence and increase growth of quality in writing. That doesn't mean that classrooms should be without negative response—for if writing is to grow, students must be able to identify and accept weaknesses. I believe that children of all ages CAN learn to give and receive honest reactions of all kinds. These are my suggestions for turning kids into loving, effective critics:

1. BUILD A SPIRIT OF KIND HELPFULNESS.
   When you begin the process of responding to writing, clarify the purposes: learning, growing, supporting.

   Talk about feelings: how hard it is to be criticized, how tearing-down statements hurt, how sensitive people may be about what they've written.

   Talk about tact: about how "I think the ending would be funnier if . . ." is easier to take than, "The ending is dumb."

   Talk about how <u>everybody's</u> writing is helped when people examine one person's work.

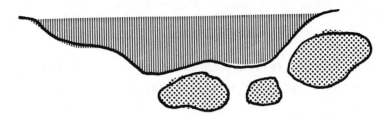

2. GIVE DIRECTION FOR THE CRITICISM.

It's a very difficult task to respond to every aspect of a whole piece! Teach kids to be effective responders by telling them what to notice:

"Find the sentence that's the funniest."

"Point out two words that are especially descriptive."

"Tell the writer what's good about the opening."

"Are there any lines in the poem that aren't clear?"

"Suggest one thing that might be added to make the tale more suspenseful."

Even VERY YOUNG children can listen or look for one colorful word or the most exciting sentence or the scariest phrase.

3. EASE INTO IT!

Start small. Have the whole group or small groups read—then respond to just a few things. Start with anonymous pieces (or let them criticize one of yours), then gradually move toward using parts or wholes of their own writing.

4. FOCUS ON THE POSITIVE.

At the beginning (maybe the first five or ten times you write) allow only positive response:

"Tell the author what words were most unusual."

"Tell the writer what he or she did best in the article."

Then move toward the responses that suggest change:

"Today, as a committee, compliment each author on one thing done very well and give one suggestion for change."

103

5. BE SPECIFIC IN THE RESPONSE. (You and the other kids)

Comments such as these say nothing:

"Lovely poem!"
"Great improvement!"
"Oh, thank you Julie, that was nice."
"What a scary story!"
"I liked it!"
"Your jokes are funny."
"Good ending!"
"Write more."

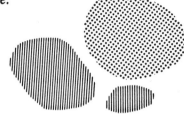

These are substantive and constructive:

"I wish your article had told more about the victims."

"The second sentence is confusing. Could you tell how he got into the castle?"

"The name you chose for the villain was really sinister!"

"I liked the way you ended with that surprise!"

"You chose interesting words to describe your puppy."

"One more sentence—maybe telling his feelings about being found—would really finish it off!"

"How about changing the word 'walked' to 'stumbled'?"

"I don't think your autobiography says enough about your family."

"It was a good idea to string all those words together—it made the girl seem very much in a hurry."

Remember that writing is a practical life skill, a tool for communicating. So ask the questions that stretch thinking, and make right-to-the-point suggestions that will improve the next writing.

TEACHING KIDS (OF ANY AGE) TO EDIT AND REVISE

EDIT: to assemble by cutting and rearranging
REVISE: to look it over again in order to amend or improve

As a fourth grade teacher, I consistently and conscientiously asked students, "Did you proofread your paper?" It took me years of reading those "Oh, yes, Mrs. Frank" papers to face the reality that their proofreading (if indeed they did it at all) was in vain. How could they in fact proofread when I had never explained what that meant? And how could they edit when nobody had ever really shown them how to cut and rearrange or told them how to amend or what to improve?

I believe there is a paucity of experience for kids in true editing --not because we are irresponsible or awful teachers, but because we have been too busy or too unsure to show them how! Part of my lack of teaching editing skills was due to disbelief. I didn't really believe little kids to be capable of identifying the kinds of improvements that I could suggest! And was I ever wrong! I'm still embarrassed by the meagerness of my faith.

THEY CAN DO IT! Let me suggest some tips for teaching editing and a way to get them started.

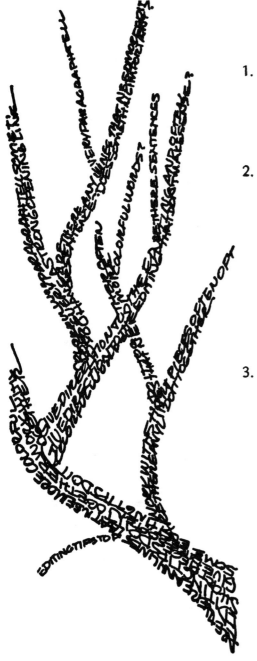

1. DO IT TOGETHER.
    Especially at the beginning, and again each time you go on to more complex editing, take the writers carefully through those responding-revising stages.

2. WORK WITH SHORT PIECES . . . OFTEN.
    Have you tried to wade through and point out all the errors and weaknesses in a sixth grader's ten-page life story? Of course you sixth grade teachers have! It's a bewildering task to edit such a long piece. A paragraph or two are much easier to handle in a limited time period—and are much more suitable for tackling one or two areas needing alteration. Even when students get on into reworking whole pieces, it's a good idea to come back to the short ones for work on specific editing skills.

3. GIVE DIRECTION TO THE EDITING.
    As with the criticism stage, when kids are editing alone or in groups, provide examples of the kinds of strengths and weaknesses to notice:
    "Are there any sentences that don't make sense?"
    "Do you have a strong opening line or sentence?"
    "Does every paragraph tell something important?"
    "Are there any lines that need more colorful words?"
    "Could someone repeat the experiment by following your notes?"
    "Check to see that you haven't begun more than three sentences with the same word."

4. DECIDE WHAT TECHNIQUES NEED TO BE REFINED.

Make a list of the writing problems that need to be attacked and the devices that should be strengthened. Add to this list as you watch their writing and notice other needs surfacing. Then choose one or two of these for work during an editing session. Obviously, certain kinds of written forms fit best with certain techniques: for example, the writing of news articles is a session ready-made for working on creating strong titles. The refinement of a writing technique is most relevant to students when the form of the piece dictates the need for working on it!

5. PUT THE EDITING EXPERIENCE TO USE IN THE NEXT WRITING.

Recall those specific learnings from one editing session when they will contribute to improvement in later writing:

"Remember those lines from last week's city poems that were so awkward because the rhyme had been forced? Let me read you a few. Now here they are after we dropped the rhyme or rearranged the lines. When you write poetry today, try to use rhyme only when it doesn't confine you or spoil the meaning of the lines."

6. DON'T OVERDO IT!

Kids need to learn when NOT to revise, too. If change is over-emphasized, they may start looking to tear apart everything; they may be inclined to spoil the fresh taste of phrases by chewing them too thoroughly. DO keep the identification of strengths within the original draft as a major focus.

...... A WAY TO BEGIN EDITING

START ... by revising an anonymous piece (something written by
you or by kids in previous classes):

"Are all the lines necessary?"

"What would be a good title for this anecdote?"

"Which words help to set a lazy mood?"

"Could you add any other lazy words?"

Do this several times, each time focusing on a few
questions.

THEN .... give anonymous pieces to small committees ALONG
WITH directions concerning one or two things to react
to and revise.

NEXT .... Pull some pieces (lines, sentences, phrases) from their
work and put them on the board or overhead projector.
As a group, respond to these:

*"Here are some sentences from the mysteries we wrote
yesterday."*

"Which words are the creepiest?"

"Which sentences add most to the mystery-feeling?"

"Are there any really bewitching words NOT used here?"

*"Do you see any places we could add a scary word to
make a sentence even more eerie?"*

*"Now look at your own mystery with your partner. See
if you can each add three more words or phrases that
will make some of your sentences more mysterious or
frightening."*

Do this kind of exercise often with groups or the whole
class.

THEN .... use their own writing. While working in pairs or small
editing groups, ask students to look for, suggest, reinforce and revise within one or two areas of need.

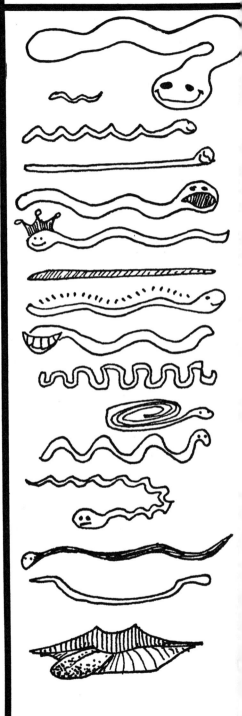

I like worms...
Big worms,
Little worms,
~~Fat~~ Fast worms,
~~Thin~~ slow worms,
~~Fast~~ sassy worms,
~~Slow~~ Flashy worms,
Dull worms,
Glow worms ——
Worms that giggle
~~Worms that~~ As they wiggle,
Worms that curl
And Worms that hump,
Worms that scurry
~~Worms that~~ In a hurry,
Worms that slither
Worms that slump.
One kind of worm,
I say with haste,
I ~~don't much~~ DO NOT like
Is a worm with taste!
(UGH)

I like worms...
Big worms,
Little worms,
Fast worms,
Slow worms,
Sassy worms,
Flashy worms,
Dull worms,
Glow worms –
Worms that giggle
As they wiggle,
Worms that curl
And worms that hump,
Worms that scurry
In a hurry,
Worms that slither
Worms that slump.

BUT

One kind of worm,
I say with haste,
I DO NOT like
Is a worm with taste!

by Shana M.
Grade 3

... substituting stronger words (more colorful, specific, etc.)
... rearranging words within a sentence
... expanding sentences
... cutting apart a short paragraph to reshuffle sentences for a different sound or meaning
... making up better titles
... changing endings
... adding one detail to the ad or article or story

Mud   Eddy
It feels so good to put your toes in mud. Mud slops and plops. It sticks to your feet. goosh goes mud. You can make mud !
mud !
mud !

Mud   Eddy
It feels so good to put your toes in slimy, gooey mud. Mud slops and plops and drops and glops. It sticks to your feet and runs through your fingers. "Goosh," goes mud. You can make mud !
mud !
mud !

WITH OLDER KIDS OR MORE EXPERIENCED WRITERS . . . .
work toward:

- . . . revising whole pieces
- . . . coordinating ideas within paragraphs
- . . . varying sentence length and structure
- . . . examining word use, using specific and/or vivid words
- . . . eliminating overused words and expressions
- . . . making effective transitions
- . . . appealing to specific audiences
- . . adapting form and style to a particular purpose
- . . . inventing exciting beginnings and strong conclusions
- . . . creating moods
- . . . incorporating dialogue into the writing
- . . . arranging details in logical order
- . . . supporting statements with specific details
- . . . eliminating unimportant words or phrases

Headache

A headache never has difficulty finding a home. A toothache has to hope for a vacancy in a holey molar. An earache waits for a cold day and chases down hatless children. Even if an earache is lucky enough to catch an ear, he has the most cramped quarters to live in. Neither a toothache nor an earache has as much room as I have. I don't have to put up with either bad breath or sticky wax. I can find a home in any head that has a problem (and most people have plenty of problems!) I've lived in some of the best heads. I have known movie stars, presidents and athletes personally. I've met more people than anybody I know but the one I wish I had never known is the one who invented aspirin!

Pat Gyer
Grade 8

The Advantages of Being a Headache

A headache never has difficulty finding a good home. A toothache has to hope for a vacancy in a holey molar. An earache must wait for a cold day to chase down hatless children. But I just move into a head any time.

Even if an earache is lucky enough to catch an ear, he has the most cramped quarters in which to live. And imagine how confining it is to be a toothache trapped inside a bicuspid! Neither has as much room as I. And I don't have to tolerate either bad breath or sticky yellow wax!

I can easily find lodging in any head that has a problem (and most people have plenty of problems!) Why, I've lived in some of the best heads! Presidents, movie stars, and even athletes, I've known personally.

I've met more people than any other ache around, but the person I wish I'd never met is the one who invented aspirin!

Pat Gyer
Grade 8

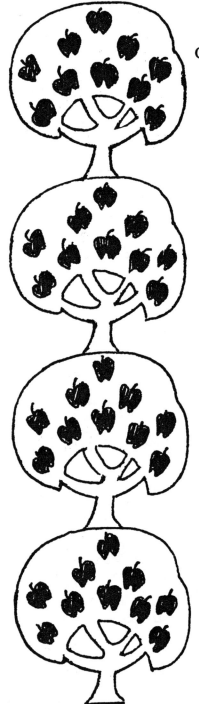

BIAS #14   *THE TOOLS OF WRITING ARE NOT THE WRITING*

The mechanical tools are necessary for effective writing, but, by themselves, do not communicate. The message is of primary importance; the structure and grammar and spelling are aides to make the message clear. Teachers and students must take care not to confuse the tools with the writing.

If a student knows that her writing will be evaluated with heavy emphasis on mechanics and spelling, she will:

use only words she's sure she can spell

keep sentences simple to avoid making mistakes

avoid any unusual punctuation situations

stick to ordinary structure

all of which adds up to NO risk, NO stretching, LITTLE growth, and even LESS excitement or discovery.

If a student has the freedom to write and write and write . . .

knowing he can go back later to change and correct

knowing he'll have help with the fixing

knowing his ideas are more important than mechanics

knowing he'll not be branded "slow" or "dumb" or

"failure" if he needs to re-write

then he can take the chances that will lead to growth in his writing.

So_____

1. **SPARE THE RED PEN!** Instead . . .
   Use a pencil to mark errors (it can be erased!).
   Make your suggestions on a separate scrap of paper.
   Keep a card file, noting misspelled words for each student. (Add those to his spelling list next week.)
   Sit with individuals or small groups and point out errors.

2. **TEACH THEM TO DO THE CHECKING.**
   Follow the pattern recommended for editing content. Begin with the whole group identifying and correcting structural or mechanical problems. Then give correcting tasks to students in pairs or small groups:
   "How many run-on sentences can your committee find?"

3. **IDENTIFY MECHANICAL SKILLS AND GRADUALLY INCLUDE THEM.**
   Make a list of the skills needed at your grade level. Add to that any apparent weaknesses you notice in their writing. Watch for chances to reinforce those skills, one at a time, during re-writing sessions.

4. **RETURN TO THOSE SKILLS IN LATER ASSIGNMENTS.**
   Once they've repaired mistakes of one kind, make use of that learning in future writing—preferably soon!
   "Today when you write, BEWARE of run-on sentences!"

5. **TALK ABOUT MISTAKES AS A NORMAL PART OF THE PROCESS.**
   Often the kid who has to correct thinks that means he's a poor writer. Make it clear that writers work constantly with dictionaries and grammar books—that fixing is just part of writing!

You'll find that your students can become good fixers of their own material. As they gain experience in editing and publishing, they begin to care. Spelling and grammar become important—and they ask for help!

EVALUATION WITHOUT EGO-DESTRUCTION

EVALUATION: to determine the worth of

Oooh . . . now this is the hard one—assigning value to a piece of writing! And before I share my ideas about evaluation, I need to bare some thoughts about how the quality of writing grows:

BIAS #15   EXPOSURE BUILDS TASTE AND QUALITY

The constant reading and sharing of writing—with consistent attention drawn to the writer's techniques and effective means of expression—brings students gradually to a sense of what constitutes good writing.

When kids write again and again . . . and react to and re-do their own and others' pieces . . . and come into contact with many examples of clear communication, they begin to absorb those concepts of what works well, what sounds pleasing, what makes sense—and with time, they begin to submit to those concepts in their own writing.

You CAN'T <u>give</u> a child a sense of taste or an eye for what's good. You CAN help him acquire it by

   . . . asking questions and drawing attention to effective means of
       communication.
   . . . giving a pattern for working and editing.
   . . . providing directions that challenge and excite.
   . . . being close by while he's learning the process.
   . . . supporting and building the <u>person</u> who is the writer.

So what is a teacher's part in evaluation? I believe that, as a teacher, I cannot and should not assign VALUE to any given piece. How can I say, "this idea is a bad one" or "this thought is worthwhile?"

> ### BIAS #16   THE TEACHER IS NOT THE FINAL CRITIC
>
> *It is the teacher's job to help the writer during the process—to help her develop the best work possible—to give aid while it's in unfinished form—NOT to judge the final product.*

Evaluation is going on throughout all the stages: when he chooses which impressions to include, as she identifies the strong parts and casts out the weak phrases, when he decides to present or not to present the finished work. And the teacher is a catalyst and a helper in that evaluation along the way. It's too late (and of little help) for the teacher to say, of the final piece, "Good," "Poor," or "Average."

Who is the final critic? I believe there are two: the student's comfort with his own work, and LIFE—the current and eventual effectiveness of his communication.

I've maintained that you can't say, "worthy" or "worthless" about a writing effort.

But you CAN say:

> *"I think this shows off your sense of humor better than anything else of yours I've read!"*
>
> *"What will you do differently next time?"*
>
> *"How do you feel about this? What did you do best?"*
>
> *"The strongest aspect is the realness of the main character."*
>
> *"Are you as satisfied with this as with your recipe book?"*
>
> *"I hope you'll continue making such good use of the class word collections in your writing."*
>
> *"I'd like to see you develop this one further."*

and you CAN:

1. HELP KIDS EVALUATE THEIR OWN.

   Keep everything they write and let them compare today's to earlier works. Ask questions that lead them to identify improvements or recurring weaknesses.

2. AVOID FALSE PRAISE.

   Refrain from, "Oh, this is wonderful!" when both you and she know it's not one of her best. Instead, point out strengths. Ask, "Why aren't you happy with this one?" And try to help her choose a particular ailment or method to work on next time she writes.

3. ELEVATE EGOS.

   Support and reinforce self-worth and self-sufficiency. No one piece of writing is important enough that its imperfections should be allowed to injure a sense of adequacy. The time spent building confidence will be time spent improving the quality of writing.

4. BE AWARE THAT, IN HIS WRITING, THE CHILD SENDS FORTH HIMSELF.

   It shouldn't be to battle. He should be sure, before he writes, that you're his ally.

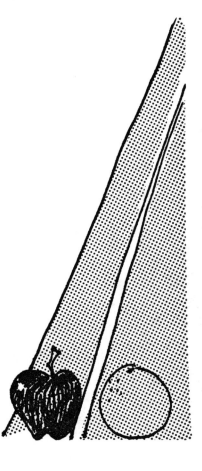

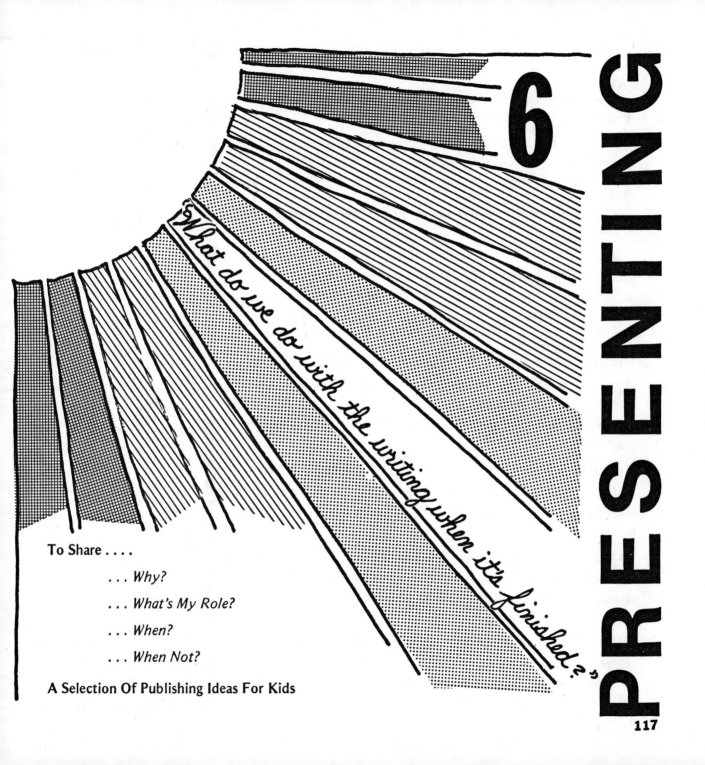

"What do we do with the writing when it's finished?"

6

PRESENTING

To Share . . . .

    . . . *Why?*

    . . . *What's My Role?*

    . . . *When?*

    . . . *When Not?*

A Selection Of Publishing Ideas For Kids

TO SHARE . . . . . .

> ### BIAS #17 PUBLICIZING ADDS DIGNITY
>
> *Making a piece of writing public advertises the importance of the writer, of his thoughts and beliefs, of her efforts. Kids should have an opportunity to share EVERY finished draft.*

✱ *WHY?*   Because . . .

— SHARING *IS* COMMUNICATING. After all . . . one of the author's most compelling motivations for the labor of reworking and refining is the preparation of a personal statement for presentation to other human beings.

— SHARING GETS WRITING OUT INTO THE LIGHT. That act of presenting it . . . of hearing it . . . of watching it live . . . of perceiving others' reactions to it . . . provides the writer with a clearer view of his work—AND influences the shape of the next work.

— SHARING INCREASES TECHNICAL ACCURACY. As kids write and publish they become spontaneously concerned about grammar and spelling and structure—and they develop as independent critics.

— SHARING ADVANCES THE CRAFT OF WRITING. If it is conscientiously used as a time for a close scrutiny of specific approaches, the sharing setting is an excellent one for elevating the techniques of writing.

— SHARING BUILDS SELF-ESTEEM. The fulfillment and self-respect a person feels upon bringing everything together into finished form are strengthened by the positive responses of others.

118

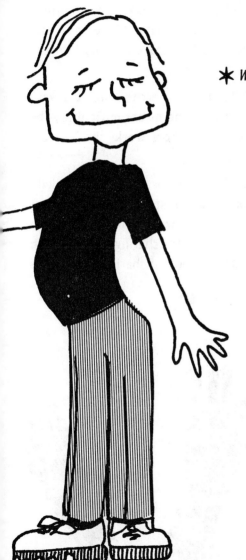

✳ WHAT'S MY ROLE?　　　　　As teacher, you're there . . .

— to PROVIDE THE TIME. Making time for them to share their writing shows you attach importance to it—and that will increase the dignity afforded writing by the students.

— to TREAT THEIR WRITING WITH RESPECT. It's a privilege if students share their personal writing with you—and they will only if they trust you as someone who listens and cares about them and their writing.

— to USE THEIR WRITING AS TOOLS FOR ADVANCING WRITING SKILLS. As they share, point out the word usages and structural devices that make for effective writing:

"Did you notice that Jamie repeated the word 'whisper' four times? What effect did that have?"

"The whole group looked scared when Jill read the phrase . . ."

"What words did Angie use to create a suspenseful mood?"

"What feeling did you get from that whole group of very short statements at the beginning of Bill's play?"

— to OFFER ACCESS TO MANY MODES OF SHARING. Just "reading your story to the class" can be confining and threatening. Let students know about enough possibilities to fit lots of different written forms and writer personalities. Then help individuals select options to fit their topics and personal styles.

✳ WHEN?

— ANYTIME . . . ANYWHERE . . . There is no one time or place for sharing. The locations and hours are unlimited in possibility. Both are best determined by the topic and form of the writing, as well as the classroom schedule. Some pieces are good morning openers. Others are best saved for rainy days. There are pieces which beg to be read aloud, while others make their best impact when presented to the eyes of the reader.

— WHEN THE WRITER WANTS TO . . . Writers don't always want to share. Nevertheless the time and means must always be available, so the writer can show off those works she feels are ready for the public.

— AS SOON AS POSSIBLE . . . Plan time for publicizing immediately upon finishing—while excitement is still high and the spirit of the experience surrounds the group with courage. Often the need, the bravery and the enthusiasm for sharing wear off with too much time. Lengthy postponement of sharing also shouts the message, "This isn't important!"

✱ WHEN NOT?

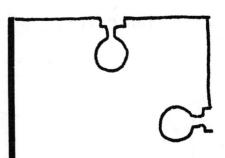

— BEFORE PRIVATE RE-READING ... Students should always be given the option of reading and re-writing BEFORE sharing. I can remember extreme discomfort at being commanded to read as soon as I'd finished something—before I was even sure I liked it!

— WHEN A STUDENT DOESN'T WANT TO ... Sharing should never be forced. Publication is for the author to choose or refuse. I guarantee my students the privacy of any works they submit, and promise never to read anything aloud without permission.

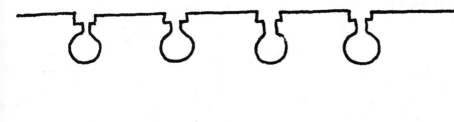

There certainly are some coaxing techniques for you to use when you sense that a student would perhaps like to share but is lacking in confidence. You can

.. Provide non-threatening ways to share. (Means that don't involve standing in front of a large group.)

.. Encourage the student to let you read it anonymously. Once she sees it accepted, she may lose some of the reservation.

.. Let him "share" it with a tape recorder, a row of dolls, some kids who are much younger, or another "easy" audience.

.. Create a mode for PRIVATE sharing such as a PRIVATE DRAWER where students may submit things without names— only for your reading.

.. Help her ease into sharing by finding one person (other than you) that she trusts enough to begin on the "making public" process.

A SELECTION OF PUBLISHING IDEAS FOR KIDS

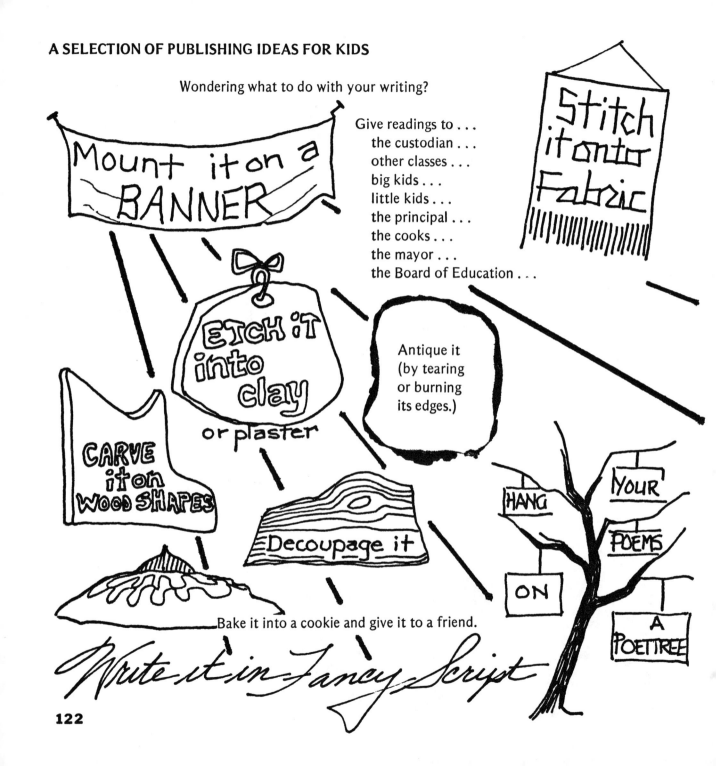

Wondering what to do with your writing?

Give readings to . . .
the custodian . . .
other classes . . .
big kids . . .
little kids . . .
the principal . . .
the cooks . . .
the mayor . . .
the Board of Education . . .

Stitch it onto Fabric

Mount it on a BANNER

ETCH IT into clay or plaster

Antique it (by tearing or burning its edges.)

CARVE it on WOOD SHAPES

Decoupage it

HANG YOUR POEMS ON A POET TREE

Bake it into a cookie and give it to a friend.

Write it in Fancy Script

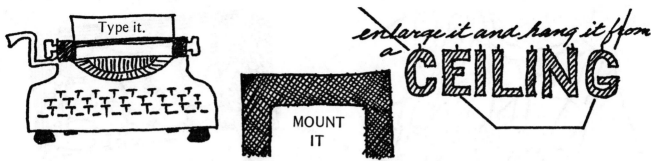

Type it.

enlarge it and hang it from a CEILING

MOUNT IT

Ditto it. Ditto it. Ditto it. Ditto it. Ditto it. Ditto it. Ditto it. Ditto it. Ditto it. Ditto it. Ditto it.

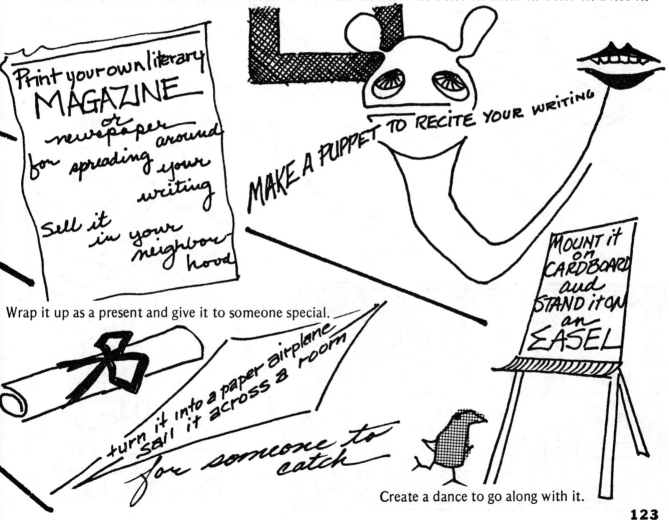

Print your own literary MAGAZINE or newspaper for spreading around your writing

Sell it in your neighborhood

MAKE A PUPPET TO RECITE YOUR WRITING

MOUNT it on CARDBOARD and STAND it on an EASEL

Wrap it up as a present and give it to someone special.

turn it into a paper airplane sail it across a room for someone to catch

Create a dance to go along with it.

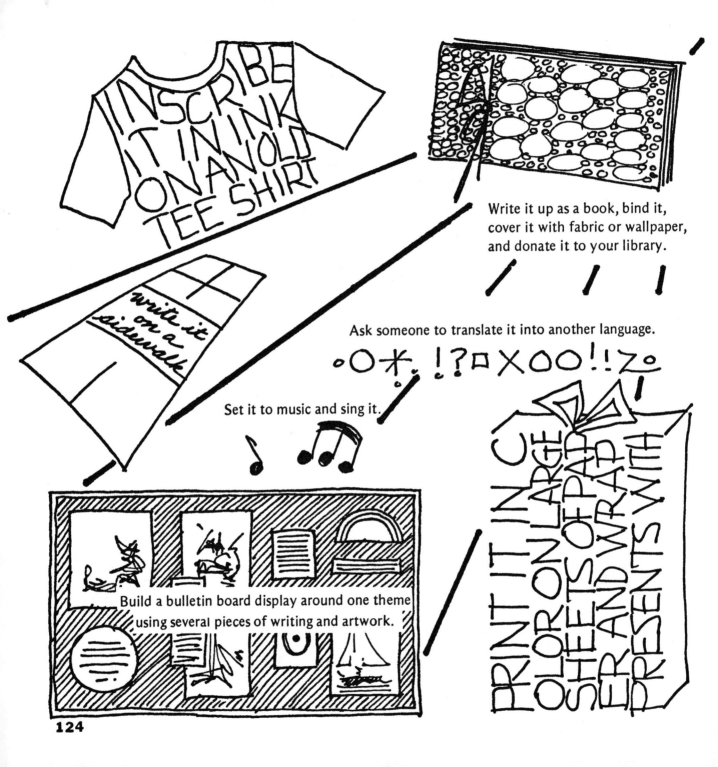

INSCRIBE IT IN INK ON AN OLD TEE SHIRT

Write it up as a book, bind it, cover it with fabric or wallpaper, and donate it to your library.

write it on a sidewalk

Ask someone to translate it into another language.

Set it to music and sing it.

Build a bulletin board display around one theme using several pieces of writing and artwork.

PRINT IT IN COLOR ON LARGE SHEETS OF PAPER AND WRAP PRESENTS WITH

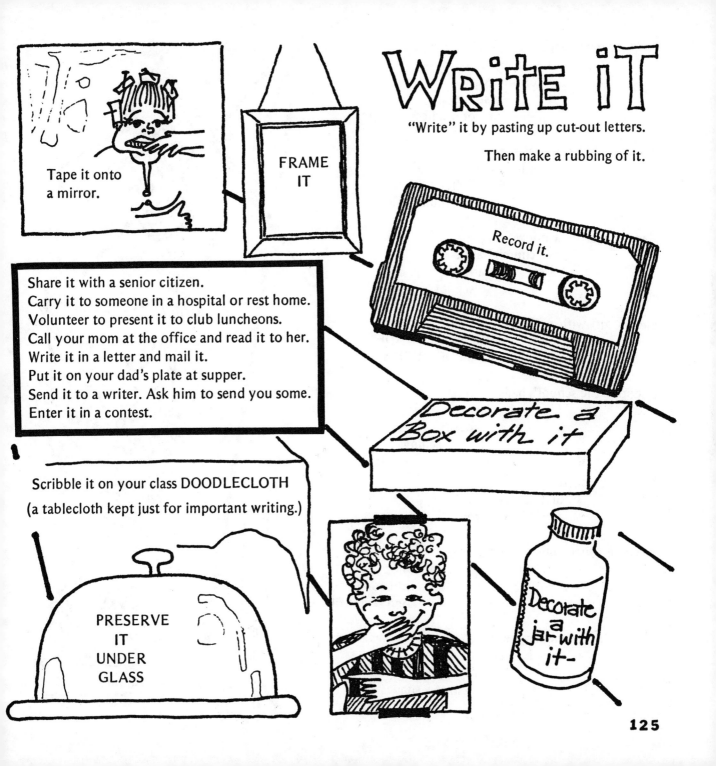

Write it

"Write" it by pasting up cut-out letters.

Then make a rubbing of it.

Tape it onto a mirror.

FRAME IT

Record it.

Share it with a senior citizen.
Carry it to someone in a hospital or rest home.
Volunteer to present it to club luncheons.
Call your mom at the office and read it to her.
Write it in a letter and mail it.
Put it on your dad's plate at supper.
Send it to a writer. Ask him to send you some.
Enter it in a contest.

Decorate a Box with it

Scribble it on your class DOODLECLOTH

(a tablecloth kept just for important writing.)

PRESERVE IT UNDER GLASS

Decorate a jar with it-

Paint it on wallpaper . . .
    or newspaper . . .
      or bricks . . .
        or stones . . .
          or old license plates

Publish it in a class newspaper . . .
      school paper . . .
        PTA bulletin . . .
          community flier

Hang it in store windows . . .
     church halls . . .
       libraries . . .
         school buses . . .

Show it off with a POETRY PARTY . . .
      a POETRY PARADE . . .
      a POETRY DAY . . .

Decorate the school's halls . . .
      walls . . .
        doors . . .
          ceilings . . .
            windows . . .

Write it on posters . . .
    billboards . . .
      blackboards . . .

Keep personal collections in a diary . . .
        or a portfolio . . .
         or a notebook . . .
           or a secret file . . .

Hang it from venetian blinds . . .
      hangers . . .
       a clothesline . . .
        window shades . . .
         door frames . . .

Put it on a flag

Make a mask that fits the writing. Wear the mask while you share it

Change it into a drama— and film it.

Write it up as a collection called "My Memoirs" and stash it away to read in ten years.

Memorize it and recite it to some friends.

Use it to start an ADD-ANOTHER-ONE collection for the class writing center.

Join a writer's caucus so that you can enjoy and exchange with other writers.

Read it, accompanied by a gymnastic routine, as a halftime show at an athletic event.

Find (or produce) a piece of art to match the theme of your work.

Read it while someone creates sound effects or does a pantomime.

Create a shadow show to present while someone reads it.

Attach it to a helium balloon and set it free!

Space for more good ideas:

Transfer it to a wall-sized mural.

Scrawl it anonymously on a graffiti mural

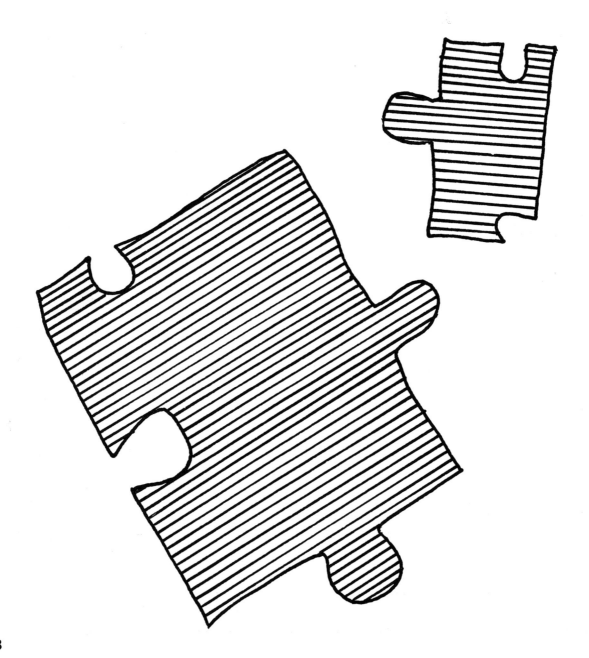

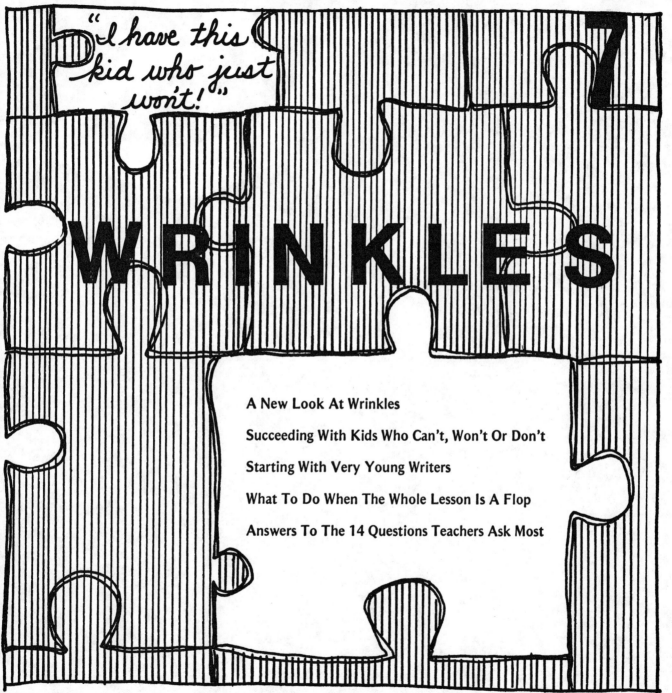

"I have this kid who just won't!"

WRINKLES

7

A New Look At Wrinkles

Succeeding With Kids Who Can't, Won't Or Don't

Starting With Very Young Writers

What To Do When The Whole Lesson Is A Flop

Answers To The 14 Questions Teachers Ask Most

WHAT DON'T YOU LIKE ABOUT WRITING?

"When the teacher reads mine out loud."

"There's never enough time to finish."

"Dumb assignments."

"Never getting our papers back."

"Fixing all the mistakes."

"When we have to pick a topic off the board and I don't like any of the topics."

"When the teacher just says, 'Write a poem,' I can't think of anything."

"When you get a grade on it and you don't know why you got that grade."

"Every time we go on a field trip we have to write a story about it when we get back. It spoils the whole trip."

"I know what I want to say but it just doesn't come out right on paper."

"Sometimes I don't feel like it but we have to anyway."

"If you write what you really think, you get in trouble."

"It's embarrassing to read what you wrote to the class."

"Getting my paper back all marked up."

"Too boring!"

"Too hard!"

"I'm no good at it."

TELL ME ABOUT THE TIMES WHEN YOU DO LIKE TO WRITE

" . . . in the morning."

"When I don't have to sign my name."

"When it doesn't have to be real long."

"When the teacher helps us get ideas and get started."

"I like to write when we're allowed to write about anything we want."

"It's better to write in class instead of for homework."

"When the teacher reads to us first."

"I like getting help with fixing mistakes."

"Writing with a friend."

"Listening to each other's writing."

"When we write about ourselves."

"When it doesn't get graded."

"When I write letters to my friends."

"When it doesn't have to rhyme."

A NEW LOOK AT WRINKLES

I suspect that you, too, have prodded the reluctant, confronted the disinterested and winced at repeated claims of, "I can't think of anything!" There are wrinkles—places and times when writing attempts don't proceed smoothly or your lessons don't go according to plan—in every classroom. The comments on the previous two pages were solicited from kids and grown-ups to find some causes and remedies for such wrinkles. They reveal the common fears, hesitations and frustrations, as well as some of the success feelings, experienced by writers.

This chapter is a place for YOU to turn when you encounter the rough spots and resistances. Its sections offer aids for working with individuals who are just beginning to write

who think they can't write

who've had little success with writing

OR who just don't want to write.

In addition, you'll find some thoughts and emergency measures for those days when nothing goes right in writing sessions and the answers to questions I'm asked most often by teachers of writing.

The place to begin is with your own view of those quirks and kinks in the writing-with-kids process. I believe you'll find more speedy successes in dealing with the difficulties if you'll consider . . .

. . . . . . that WRINKLES ARE NORMAL.

Everybody has periods of laziness and self-consciousness and disinterest in writing. I've had them all! There have been weeks when I didn't care if I ever finished this book, even though I believe strongly in the ideas and am committed to the writing of it. And sometimes a chapter has lain finished many days before I could bear to present it to my editor—because I get embarrassed when people read what I write! I believe you're in for frustrations if you expect every student to be anxious to write during every writing session OR if you even expect yourself to be enthused each time.

. . . . . . that WRINKLES MAY NOT BE WRINKLES AT ALL.

Frequently a student's apparent lack of success is only her lack of being on the same step of the ladder as someone else. There are so many levels of writing ability that, in any one group, there are bound to be vast differences in kind, quality and complexity of finished products. Take care not to see differences as problems.

. . . . . . that WRINKLES ARE DESIRABLE.

If diversity is honored, then resistance to writing in one form or on a given topic will be welcomed. A writing session produces higher quality work when students are free to pursue options other than the initial suggestion. The discontent of one student with an assignment just may be the stimulus that propels the writer off in a better direction OR generates ten new ideas OR stretches your mind to create an alternative. Often the lessons that "don't work" are the very ones that give birth to the most exhilarating and productive results.

SUCCEEDING WITH KIDS WHO CAN'T, WON'T OR DON'T

Most likely you WILL encounter students who, out of fear, undeveloped motor skills, boredom, disbelief, stubbornness or weariness—will be unwilling or unable to write. One or two or several or all of these suggestions may help you to live comfortably with such incidents and/or to woo such individuals to successful writing.

1. CONCENTRATE FIRST ON PEOPLE-BUILDING!

    Good feelings about self increase willingness to express that self. Any time dedicated to exercises that prove to kids their worth and ability will be hours spent cementing the very foundation of written expression.

2. SPEND MORE TIME ON STAGES 1 AND 2.

    It is my experience that, when kids won't write or think they can't, it is usually because they haven't been romanced. When they're stuck during writing, go back and collect more ideas, read more examples, gather more words. OR, spend several sessions JUST on the motivation and collection stages.

3. GIVE TIME OFF.

    Respect the lack of interest in a topic or the low enthusiasm on a particular day and allow individuals to NOT write. If you're offering writing experiences often, an occasional day off won't inhibit growth.

4. DON'T ANNOUNCE WRITING AHEAD OF TIME.

    For a student already nervous about writing, fears can only be compounded by a schedule that says: *Creative Writing—2:30.* She'll have the whole day to build up resistance! Sneak into it, so that before they even realize it, they're pursuing an idea and scrawling down words.

5. ENCOURAGE OTHER FORMS OF EXPRESSION.

Just as exposure to chicken pox doesn't assure catching the disease, so contact with joyful writing experience doesn't produce writing fever for all students. For some, it is not and never will be the best means of communication. Activities in art, music and movement will enable many kinds of communicators to excel and will, at the same time, strengthen written expression.

6. GO BACK TO WORDS.

Whatever your writers' ages, for all of them the foundation must be strong before the structure will be stable. If writing is difficult, return to word play for solidifying the building blocks.

7. RETURN TO THE ORAL.

Instead of WRITING in Stage 3, TALK the rough draft. Students often gain fluency and confidence by forming their thoughts into oral sentences. Once they're talking comfortably and fluently, then ease back into writing—or write for them.

8. ACCENTUATE THE SHORT.

> ### BIAS #18 SMALL IS BEAUTIFUL
> *The writing of short pieces makes success possible for more students and allows for effective teaching of writing techniques.*

It's one of my strongest biases! New or reluctant writers are more likely to succeed with small works (and are more willing to write) because the writing goes faster and there are fewer mistakes to correct. The rewards come more quickly!

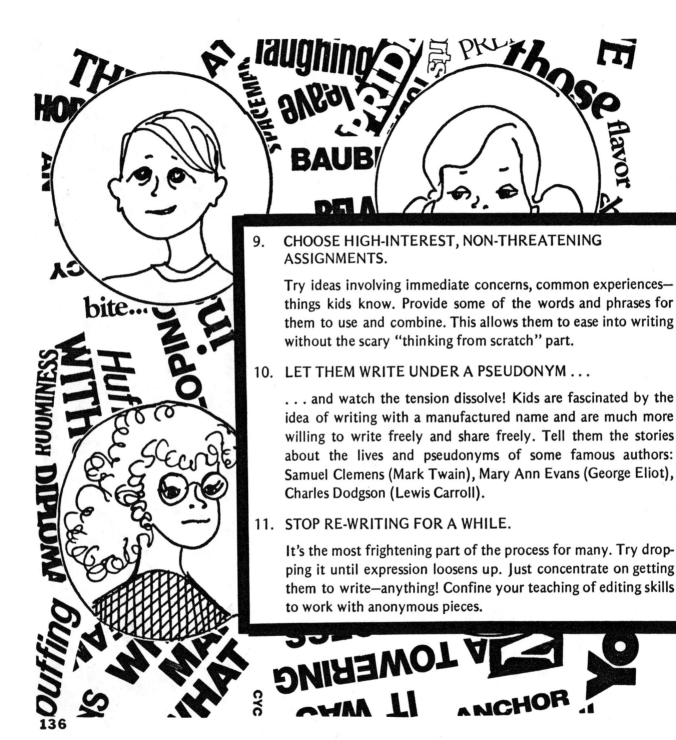

9. **CHOOSE HIGH-INTEREST, NON-THREATENING ASSIGNMENTS.**

   Try ideas involving immediate concerns, common experiences—things kids know. Provide some of the words and phrases for them to use and combine. This allows them to ease into writing without the scary "thinking from scratch" part.

10. **LET THEM WRITE UNDER A PSEUDONYM . . .**

    . . . and watch the tension dissolve! Kids are fascinated by the idea of writing with a manufactured name and are much more willing to write freely and share freely. Tell them the stories about the lives and pseudonyms of some famous authors: Samuel Clemens (Mark Twain), Mary Ann Evans (George Eliot), Charles Dodgson (Lewis Carroll).

11. **STOP RE-WRITING FOR A WHILE.**

    It's the most frightening part of the process for many. Try dropping it until expression loosens up. Just concentrate on getting them to write—anything! Confine your teaching of editing skills to work with anonymous pieces.

12. WRITE IN CLASS WHERE PLENTY OF HELP IS AVAILABLE.

Security is the key for these kids. They tend to feel lost when assistance is too far away. Go back to writing together whenever you sense your writers are struggling alone.

13. COMBINE WRITERS INTO PAIRS OR GROUPS.

It's always easier to face a tough task with company, and two brainstormers will usually produce more ideas than a lone writer. You might try asking a shy writer to assist a younger child with a writing project. This is a good tactic for building feelings of confidence and self-worth.

14. BEWARE BORING OR RIGID FORMS!

Asking a young writer to comply with a tight form (a specific rhyme pattern or number of syllables) sometimes makes the goal seem additionally unattainable. Forcing forms that have no appeal to the individual threatens what little motivation there may be already.

15. PROVIDE MORE DIRECTION.

Too many choices or too open an assignment can be confusing or frightening for unsure writers. Try giving more specifics:
"Put a color in every line . . . ,"
"Use four of the phrases from the chart."
"Start each line with . . I WOULDN'T LIKE TO _____"

16. TRY TRANSCRIPTS.

Let students tell their stories, etc. to each other while one transcribes the sentences. OR, provide a tape recorder for a student who's having difficulty with the writing. After he speaks it onto the tape, he can go back and translate the oral into written words.

STARTING WITH VERY YOUNG WRITERS

There hasn't been time for them to build fears or accumulate failures in writing! They are still awed by the magic of language. You can enjoy the delight of keeping that fresh and alive. Think of your task as one of planting the seeds. Since your writers are too young to write lengthy pieces (or to write at all!) the time is free for spreading excitement about words, showing off the talents of language and making communication easy and enjoyable.

To start the flow of expression in little kids that will lead to writing skill, try these:

.... **SENSITIZE** them to their environment. Get them to FEEL! Chew grass, catch snow, smell tacos, listen to butterflies, mimic animals, adopt different roles. Touch and taste and smell and watch and listen—and, as you do, share impressions.

.... **TALK** with them about their feelings, ideas, discoveries. They have plenty of experiences on which to draw. Ask them to talk about: *"How does a lemon taste? What does it do to your tongue?"*
"What does morning smell like?"
"How does it feel to have an ant crawl over your arm?"
"Were you ever lost? How did you feel?"

.... **TAPE RECORD** their answers to questions. Their cumulative statements and impressions will comprise a composition that can be written down by you or one of them or an older child.

.... **READ, READ, READ!** Let kids join in on refrains and short poems. Ask them to add different happenings or new endings or extra lines. Let them interpret as you read—by adding sound effects, clapping rhythms or moving their bodies.

. . . . **LISTEN** to songs, records, tapes. Sing along. Compose songs and poems together or add verses to the songs you hear. Listen for rhythms and rhymes and special words.

. . . . **COMPOSE ORALLY.** Create lots of sentences, word groups, rhymes, riddles, questions, sayings. Some of the time you can jot them down and read them back to the group. Hearing the things they've created provides proof to them that they CAN write.

. . . . **INVITE** helpers into your classroom to take dictations. Let the young students dictate to an older student, a mother, a father, the principal, a grandparent, a senior citizen—anyone who can record the original material for the young writer.

. . . . **SHOW OFF** their writing after they've dictated it to you or someone else. They love to see their compositions typed or enlarged on posters and banners. This supplies great reading material for them, too!

. . . **PAIR** each student with an older child for the purpose of creating a written piece together. Make it clear that each partner is to contribute ideas.

. . . . **EMPHASIZE** short pieces such as:

word collections	*questions*	*short letters*
phrases	*sentences*	*captions*
observations	*jokes*	*riddles*
short descriptions	*definitions*	*poems*
directions	*similes*	*titles*

. . . . **NOTICE** the word play ideas in Chapter 2. Most of those are ideal for young children and beginning writers. Notice, as well, the section in Chapter 8 that suggests ideas especially for little kids.

WHAT TO DO WHEN THE WHOLE LESSON IS A FLOP

If the products are not what you'd hoped they'd be, OR if some or all of the students are disinterested or unmotivated or unchallenged, ask yourself—and ask your kids

... *What are my expectations? Are they too high? too low?*
... *Is there something being learned in the process in spite of problems with the product?*
... *Am I smothering the joy of writing with too much rewriting?*
... *Is the assignment too wide? too narrow? Is there enough direction?*
... *Is the topic enticing and relevant?*
... *Did I treat the assignment with importance?*
... *Did I skimp on the time?*
... *Have I chosen a time when kids are otherwise occupied or tired?*
... *Was the assignment too long?*
... *Have I been providing regularly for sharing?*

THEN
     ... Modify your goals.
OR ..... Decide to concentrate on parts of the process and skip a final product for now.
OR ..... Take the topic in a different, more appealing direction.
OR ..... Ask the students to suggest another topic.
OR ..... Use the time for kids just to write freely—on any topic!
OR ..... Put it off until another time, when writers are more ready.
OR ..... Stop and do some re-circulating exercises. Then try again.
OR ..... Instead of writing, use the time to inventory kids' interests in order to suit the writing to them. Ask them to complete statements such as:
         *Things that are important to me are*_____
         *I like to read about*_____
         *I worry about*_____
         *I like to spend my time*_____
         *I wish I knew more about*_____
         *If I ever write a book it will be about*_____
OR ..... Drop the idea all together. Try a new one on another day!

ANSWERS TO THE 14 QUESTIONS TEACHERS ASK MOST

Q. How often should kids write?

A. *Some kind of writing should be happening daily. (Suggesting the keeping of a personal journal is one way to encourage daily writing.)*

I recommend a teacher-initiated or group-writing experience once a week if possible (no less than once every two weeks).

Q. I have to give a grade for creative writing on report cards. How do I decide?

A. *Keep careful records of individual difficulties.*
Examine samples of writing over a period of weeks.
Watch and note involvement in editing groups.
THEN, if you have to assign a number or A, B, C . . . grade GROWTH, PARTICIPATION IN THE WHOLE PROCESS, and WILLINGNESS TO TRY.

Q. When should you ask kids to go through the WHOLE process?

A. *Perhaps: every two or three times you write. (Some may re-work even when it's not required.)*

Also: when kids are particularly excited about a piece or for any reason are anxious to have a precise draft.

Less: with younger and reluctant writers.

More: with older or more advanced writers.

Q. When should you NOT ask kids to re-write?

A. *When the piece doesn't need it. Sometimes the first draft is final in its freshness. Help kids recognize such times!*

When you're concentrating on just one of the stages.

When an individual feels the first draft isn't worth the re-writing time.

When you need a break from re-writing for a while.

Q. How can I get my kids to tolerate fixing?

A. *The best way I know is to bring in a real live writer who will show his raw manuscripts and talk about the fixing he does.   Other good ways are:*

> *— doing it together*
> *— making it fun (ie: "Let's track down all the dull verbs! Who can find three?")*
> *— working into it in small steps*
> *— promising that they won't have to do it every time!*

Q. Do you always read everything your kids write?

A. *No! Kids should do lots of writing on their own that is shared with the teacher only if they choose. I certainly don't share all my writing with them or anybody else!*

Q. Do I have to write comments on everything they write for class assignments?

A. *NO—they may choose to keep some of the things private.*

NO—kids can serve as responders and critics for one another.

NO—often your response is given orally, casually—while looking over shoulders.

BUT—you should respond carefully and thoroughly some of the time— either in writing or in a one-to-one conference with the writer.

Q. Most of my students just don't use the writing center. How can I get them to go there?

A. *ASSIGN THEM!*

Q. Doesn't telling kids to write without stopping to correct just encourage mistakes?

A. *The hurrying-to-get-down-your-thoughts-before-you-lose-them approach doesn't instill sloppiness. The teacher isn't saying, "Make mistakes freely!" Tell kids to use the rules they know and not to make mistakes on purpose. The idea is that you don't waste precious time stopping to labor over a word you can't spell or a rule you don't remember.*

Q. What should we do with the unfinished pieces?

A. *I'm for not throwing away any writing! Because an incomplete thought today may be the nucleus for a masterpiece six months from tomorrow, it should be stored and guarded! For doing this, I suggest: a personal NOT YET PUBLISHED file into which each writer stuffs the things she or he doesn't like,*

> *gave up on,*
> *lost interest in,*
> *or wants to work on later.*

This file can become the raw material for further writing:

> *"Go through your file and find an exciting phrase that got buried in a never-finished piece. Use that phrase somewhere in the description you're writing today."*

or: *"Next Wednesday we are each going to publish one thing in a Brag Bulletin. Go through your writing file and choose one to finish. You'll have time every day between now and Tuesday to get it ready for publication."*

Q. What do you do with kids who write dirty words?

A. *I have two tactics and use whichever seems appropriate at the time:*

1) *Let them live with their own words.*
I find that kids do a lot of self-censoring or group-censoring. The objectionable words and phrases written for shock effect in the first draft usually disappear by the final draft. (Incidentally, the teacher's horrified response somehow increases the life-span of obscenities!)

2) *Threaten strangulation.*

Q. Should kids be allowed poetic license?

A. *Yes! . . . as long as they KNOW they're taking liberties. One reservation: It would be a shame for any one student to do all her writing thus. I believe students need plenty of experiences with standard forms in addition to the experimental.*

Q. What do I do if I've tried everything and a student still can't think of anything to write?

A. *Find something non-disruptive for him to do while others write*
(but DO involve him in the response stages and in listening to others who share).

OR ask her to spend the time writing private thoughts in a journal.

OR suggest that he keep a record of what the others are doing as they write.

AND stop worrying! If you have forty writing lessons during a year, and she misses half of them, she still will have had twenty valuable experiences. Besides, if she's in on the criticism, editing and fixing of others' works, she'll be growing even though she's not writing herself!

Q. What if I don't like writing? I mean, I really have a bad attitude!

A. *Don't teach it! Being without formal writing lessons for a year isn't good, but exposure to ill feelings about writing can be worse. Try anything to convert yourself to feeling good about it. If that doesn't work, ask another teacher to hold writing sessions with your kids or let students write on their own.*

Dream In Broad Daylight: 100 Alternatives To
What I Did On My Summer Vacation

Especially, But Not Only, For Little Kids

Especially, But Not Only, For Reluctant Writers

Especially, But Not Only, For Gifted Writers

Ideas For Mixing Writing With Other Content Areas

" I always run out of ideas by October ! "

JUST IDEAS

dreams

IN BROAD DAYLIGHT *100 alternatives to "what I did on my summer vacation"*

Dear Teacher,

The ideas in this chapter are directed at various kinds of kids, levels, interests and topics. For most of them you can adapt the activity to a different level by changing the examples, simplifying the directions or adding more details.

Each idea is described BRIEFLY. None is developed as thoroughly here as it would need be if used as a motivator for a writing lesson. These are beginnings—kernels. YOU add the discussion, brainstorming, dramatizing and collecting that help the kernels explode into writing!

EPITAPHS

WRITE SOME SILLY EPITAPHS:

Here lies Maryanne Doe
She tripped on a toothpick
* And broke her toe.*

At rest here is John Bloom
Our neighbor of late.
He brushed with Crest
But should've used Colgate.

CAN YOU WRITE ONE FOR:
Peter Pan?   a plumber?
a snake who got bit by a poisonous
* lady?*

FOUND WRITING

FOR ANYONE WHO DOESN'T FEEL LIKE WRITING, HERE'S A WAY TO WRITE WITHOUT WRITING! CREATE

POEMS	OR	SENTENCES
PHRASES	OR	WORDS
FABLES	OR	ANNOUNCEMENTS
LETTERS	OR	WARNINGS
NOTES	OR	QUESTIONS
STORIES	OR	SECRETS

BY CUTTING THE WORDS AND LETTERS OUT OF MAGAZINES OR NEWSPAPERS. <u>THIS IS A GREAT WAY TO SEND RANSOM NOTES OR ANONYMOUS MESSAGES.</u>

HOW TO . . .

WRITE THE DIRECTIONS FOR HOW TO:

make the sun shine
eat with chopsticks
find the washroom
get bubblegum out of your hair
brush your teeth
make a rainbow
pet a lion
cook a turkey
get peanut butter off the roof of
* your mouth*

FIRST CLASS MAIL

WHEN YOU'RE IN THE MOOD FOR WRITING A LETTER, WRITE TO . . .

. . . a celebrity . . . asking him to tell you something he's never told anyone
. . . an animal you'd like to convince to be your pet
. . . someone whose name you've chosen from your mom's address book
. . . yourself from yourself
. . . yourself as if it were coming from someone in the future
. . . an historical figure, asking some questions you wish they could've answered for you

WRITE TO THANK SOMEONE, TO APOLIGIZE, TO REQUEST, TO COMPLAIN, OR TO CHEER!

YOU'RE INVITED

WRITE AN INVITATION TO ANY SORT OF AN EVENT . . . SERIOUS OR SILLY . . . REAL OR IMAGINARY . . . IN THE PRESENT OR PAST OR FUTURE. BE SURE TO TELL THE GUESTS WHEN IT STARTS AND ENDS, WHAT TO EXPECT AND WHAT TO BRING.

Invite someone to:

a ladybug hunt
World War II
a cloud walk
a trip to tomorrow
a beheading
a safari

an archaeological dig in Egypt
a wild river raft trip
an alligator hunt
a boomerang throwing contest
the Battle of Gettysburg
totem pole building party

LOVE STORIES

WRITE ABOUT ROMANCES BETWEEN UNUSUAL PAIRS OF LOVERS:

a tennis shoe and a potato peel
a bee and a mathematician
a doctor and a bandage

TELL HOW THE RELATIONSHIP DEVELOPED.

CRAZY COMBINATIONS

WRITE A POEM THAT HAS IN EVERY LINE . . .

the name of an animal and a kitchen utensil
a color and a fruit
a body part and a famous person
a power source and a dance
OR any other crazy combination!

WRITER'S MARATHON

HAVE A MARATHON IN YOUR CLASS OR SCHOOL (OR JOIN WITH ANOTHER CLASS). SET A STARTING TIME FOR PEOPLE TO BEGIN WRITING. AGREE ON A PRIZE FOR THE PERSON WHO WRITES THE LONGEST OR FOR ANYONE WHO CAN WRITE LONGER THAN THREE HOURS. YOU'LL NEED TO MAKE UP YOUR OWN RULES TO FIT THE SCHEDULES AND AGES OF YOUR MARATHONERS.

ARE YOU TALKING TO YOURSELF?

THE NEXT TIME YOU TALK TO YOURSELF . . . LISTEN! . . . AND KEEP NOTES ON WHAT YOU'RE SAYING. WRITE YOUR CONVERSATIONS WITH YOURSELF IN THE FORM OF A DIALOGUE OR MONOLOGUE OR POEM. OR, ASK A FRIEND TO LISTEN TO YOU WHEN YOU TALK AND WRITE DOWN WHAT HE HEARS YOU SAYING.

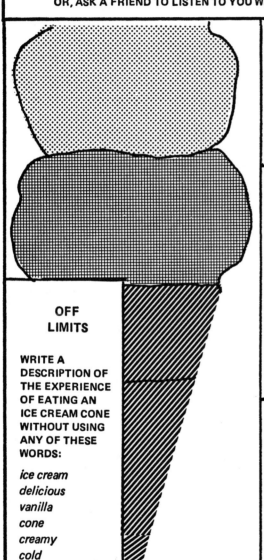

OFF LIMITS

WRITE A DESCRIPTION OF THE EXPERIENCE OF EATING AN ICE CREAM CONE WITHOUT USING ANY OF THESE WORDS:

ice cream
delicious
vanilla
cone
creamy
cold
lick
bite

COMPLAINT DEPARTMENT

PRETEND THAT YOU ARE IN CHARGE OF THE COMPLAINT DEPARTMENT AT A GROCERY STORE OR ICE CREAM PARLOR OR A KITE SHOP OR A BICYCLE REPAIR SHOP—OR ANY OTHER STORE. WRITE A LIST OF THE POSSIBLE COMPLAINTS YOU MIGHT RECEIVE. FOR EACH ONE HAVE READY A POSSIBLE ANSWER OR EXPLANATION.

COME TO YOUR SENSES!

CHOOSE A HUMAN EMOTION OR ANY OTHER IDEA. THINK ABOUT IT AND EXPERIENCE IT WITH ALL <u>FIVE SENSES.</u> WRITE A LINE THAT TELLS WHAT COLOR IT IS. THEN WRITE SOME OTHER LINES TO DESCRIBE IT USING JUST ONE OF THE SENSES.

Joy is bright green.	*(color)*
It tastes like orange juice.	*(taste)*
It smells like sunshine.	*(smell)*
And reminds me of fireworks.	*(sight)*
It sounds like a crackling fire.	*(sound)*
Joy makes me feel like giggling.	*(feel)*
	Mary Lee Fiacco, Grade 2

ON THE SPOT SPEECHES

YOU HAVE THREE MINUTES TO PREPARE FOR A ONE MINUTE SPEECH. WRITE DOWN NOTES TO YOURSELF FOR THE IDEAS OR POINTS YOU'LL WANT TO INCLUDE IN THE SPEECH. HERE ARE SOME SPEECH TOPICS:

What to do when you've swallowed a Junebug
Why a woman should be president
Ten good uses for a pocket
How to show anger without getting in trouble
The ideal school
Situations to avoid

TALL TALES

WRITE A STORY ABOUT A HAPPENING IN A WAY THAT STRETCHES THE FACTS A LITTLE OR A LOT. DO YOUR WRITING ON A PIECE OF ADDING MACHINE TAPE THAT YOU'VE TURNED THE LONG WAY. MOUNT THE TALL TALE ON BLACK PAPER AND CUT OUT LEGS FOR IT SO THAT IT IS VERY TALL.

COME AWAY WITH US

WRITE PAMPHLETS OR BROCHURES THAT WILL SELL SOMEONE ON THE IDEA OF JOINING A TRIP OR VISITING A SPECIAL PLACE:

a castle turned into a luxury hotel
a tennis camp or kids-only resort
a diet ranch, reducing salon or health spa
a raft trip down the Mississippi River
a newly-discovered volcano
Ali Baba's cave or the inside of Aladdin's lamp

CLIFF HANGERS

HANG A LONG PIECE OF PAPER FROM A HANGER. ON THE PAPER, WRITE THE BEGINNING OF AN EXCITING STORY. DON'T FINISH THE STORY! STOP RIGHT AT A BREATHTAKING SPOT. THEN HANG YOUR STORY IN A PLACE WHERE SOMEONE ELSE CAN FINISH IT. YOU FINISH ANOTHER PERSON'S CLIFF-HANGER.

EAVESDROPPING

LISTEN TO A CONVERSATION. WRITE DOWN THEIR WORDS AS ACCURATELY AS YOU CAN. DON'T TRY THIS ONE TOO OFTEN OR YOU COULD GET IN TROUBLE!

GOSSIP GALORE

WRITE A GOSSIP COLUMN ABOUT THE PEOPLE IN YOUR SCHOOL. INCLUDE ONLY THE KIND OF GOSSIP THAT WON'T HURT PEOPLE'S FEELINGS OR EMBARRASS THEM.

PERSONAL POETRY CACHE

PICK A THEME YOU LIKE OR AN AREA OF YOUR OWN INTEREST: PLANTS, SPORTS, ANIMALS, DREAMS, FEELINGS, SEASONS, MISCHIEF, NATURE, SOUNDS, ETC. COLLECT POEMS THAT RELATE TO YOUR THEME FROM POETRY BOOKS. WRITE THEM INTO A NOTEBOOK OR SCRAPBOOK THAT YOU'VE MADE. ADD AT LEAST TWO OF YOUR OWN POEMS ON THE THEME TO YOUR COLLECTION.

149

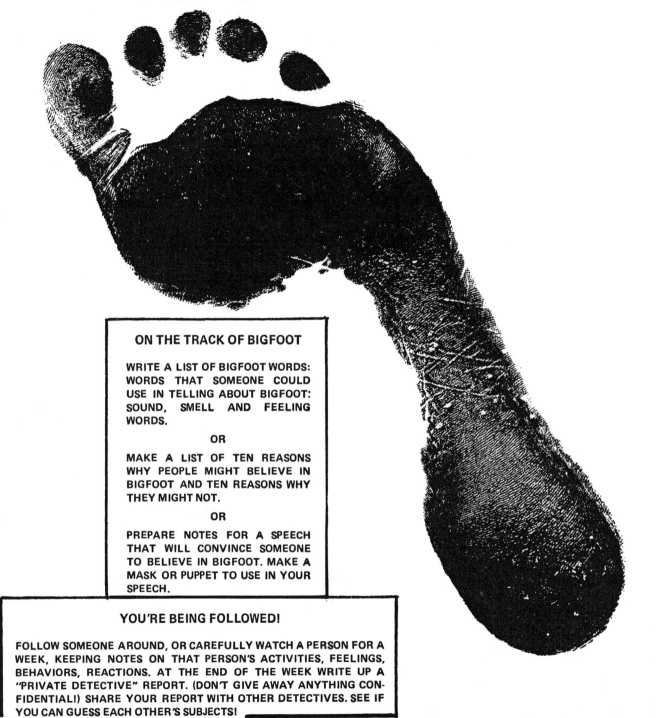

ON THE TRACK OF BIGFOOT

WRITE A LIST OF BIGFOOT WORDS: WORDS THAT SOMEONE COULD USE IN TELLING ABOUT BIGFOOT: SOUND, SMELL AND FEELING WORDS.

OR

MAKE A LIST OF TEN REASONS WHY PEOPLE MIGHT BELIEVE IN BIGFOOT AND TEN REASONS WHY THEY MIGHT NOT.

OR

PREPARE NOTES FOR A SPEECH THAT WILL CONVINCE SOMEONE TO BELIEVE IN BIGFOOT. MAKE A MASK OR PUPPET TO USE IN YOUR SPEECH.

YOU'RE BEING FOLLOWED!

FOLLOW SOMEONE AROUND, OR CAREFULLY WATCH A PERSON FOR A WEEK, KEEPING NOTES ON THAT PERSON'S ACTIVITIES, FEELINGS, BEHAVIORS, REACTIONS. AT THE END OF THE WEEK WRITE UP A "PRIVATE DETECTIVE" REPORT. (DON'T GIVE AWAY ANYTHING CONFIDENTIAL!) SHARE YOUR REPORT WITH OTHER DETECTIVES. SEE IF YOU CAN GUESS EACH OTHER'S SUBJECTS!

ODES

WRITE AN ODE TO . . .

. . . a cocoon
. . . peanut butter
. . . the pencil sharpener
. . . a super mother
. . . your old sneaker
. . . curly hair
. . . a toothbrush
. . . a rainy day
. . . the end of summer
. . . the teacher's sense of humor
. . . your childhood

RE-PRINTS

FIND A PICTURE YOU LIKE. WRITE A VERY PRECISE DESCRIPTION OF THE PICTURE. THEN TRADE DESCRIPTIONS WITH ANOTHER STUDENT. (DO NOT SHOW THE PICTURE!) ASK HER/HIM TO TRY TO RE-CREATE THE PICTURE BY DRAWING IT ACCORDING TO YOUR DESCRIPTION. (YOU TRY THE SAME WITH HIS.) THEN . . . COMPARE THE DRAWINGS WITH THE ORIGINALS!

THERE IS THIS PLACE I KNOW

CHOOSE A REAL OR IMAGINARY PLACE THAT IS A SPECIAL PLACE TO BE. (IT MAY BE PRIVATE OR PUBLIC!) MAYBE IT'S YOUR VERY FAVORITE PLACE. TELL WHAT IT IS LIKE AND WHY IT IS SPECIAL. WRITE ABOUT IT IN A PRIVATE LETTER TO A FRIEND.

DOES THE NAME FIT?

MAKE UP NAMES FOR CHARACTERS YOU SEE IN PICTURES. MAKE THE NAMES MATCH THE QUALITIES THAT YOU THINK YOU SEE.
OR
WITHOUT USING PICTURES, CREATE NAMES AND WRITE DESCRIPTIONS OF PERSONS TO FIT THE NAMES. FOR EACH NAME, TELL HOW IT HAS INFLUENCED THE PERSON'S LIFE.

WAKE UP AMERICA!

INVENT AND DESCRIBE A NEW PRODUCT THAT WOULD BE GUARANTEED TO WAKE UP ANYBODY IN THE MORNING—GENTLY BUT FIRMLY. WRITE AN ADVERTISEMENT FOR YOUR INVENTION.

LOOKING FOR TROUBLE?

WRITE WARNINGS THAT CAUTION PEOPLE AGAINST POSSIBLE HAZARDS IN YOUR SCHOOL OR AT HOME OR IN THE STREETS OR ON THE SCHOOL BUS OR AT A CIRCUS OR IN A GYM OR ANYWHERE ELSE THAT SAFETY IS IMPORTANT.

THE OTHER SIDE

PRETEND TO BE YOUR ENEMY OR A PERSON WHO IS OPPOSING YOU ON SOME IDEA. WRITE ABOUT HOW THAT PERSON SEES AND FEELS ABOUT YOU.

TREE TALK

GATHER SOME PIECES OF BARK OR CHUNKS OF WOOD OFF THE GROUND OR ASK SOMEONE TO CUT A SLAB OF WOOD FROM A DEAD LOG FOR YOU. THEN USE A PEN OR PAINTBRUSH OR FINE-POINT MARKER TO WRITE ON THE WOOD. WRITE NATURE WORDS, TREE POEMS, WOOD PHRASES OR OUTDOOR IMPRESSIONS ON THE WOOD. (TRY THIS ON OLD SHINGLES TOO!)

WANTED

MAKE A POSTER DESCRIBING A PERSON WHO IS MISSING. TELL ABOUT THE PERSON'S PHYSICAL CHARACTERISTICS AND HABITS. EXPLAIN WHY HE/SHE IS MISSING AND SUGGEST THE KINDS OF PLACES THE PERSON MIGHT BE LIKELY TO BE FOUND. DRAW OR CUT OUT A PICTURE FOR THE POSTER.

APOLOGIES

This Is Just To Say

*I have eaten
the plums
that were in
the icebox*

*and which
you were probably
saving
for breakfast*

*Forgive me
they were delicious
so sweet
and so cold.*

William Carlos Williams

HAVE YOU EVER APOLOGIZED FOR SOMETHING FOR WHICH YOU WEREN'T REALLY SORRY?

WRITE A POEM OR NOTE THAT GIVES AN APOLOGY FOR SOMETHING YOU'VE DONE.

*The baseball
has broken
your dining room
window*

*and I know
you're having company
for dinner.*

*Forgive me
it was a fine hit
and I got
a home run.*

Steven Phoenix Grade 4

BITS OF WISDOM

AT THE END OF A SCHOOL YEAR, WRITE A SHORT NOTE OF COMMENT OR ADVICE TO EACH PERSON IN YOUR CLASS, TELLING THAT PERSON SOMETHING IMPORTANT OR HELPFUL FOR HIM TO KNOW OR REMEMBER AS HE GOES ON IN LIFE. DON'T FORGET THE TEACHER!

BORROWED STARTERS

BORROW A LINE FROM A POEM OR A TITLE FROM A BOOK TO SERVE AS THE STARTING LINE FOR YOUR OWN STORY OR MOVIE SCRIPT OR POEM OR DESCRIPTION.

DIAMANTE

A DIAMANTE IS A DIAMOND-SHAPED POEM THAT TELLS ABOUT OPPOSITES. START WITH A PAIR OF OPPOSITES SUCH AS DAY-NIGHT, NEW-OLD, ETC.

LINES 1 AND 7 NAME THE OPPOSITES.
LINES 2 AND 6 EACH GIVE TWO ADJECTIVES DESCRIBING THE OPPOSITE NEAREST IT.
LINES 3 AND 5 GIVE THREE PARTICIPLES (ING WORDS) DESCRIBING THE NEAREST OPPOSITE. LINE 4 IS IN THE MIDDLE. IT CHANGES FROM THE FIRST IDEA TO THE OPPOSITE BY GIVING TWO NOUNS FOR EACH. SEE THE EXAMPLE BELOW. NOTICE HOW THE POEM CHANGES FROM ONE THEME TO THE OPPOSITE:

DAY
Bright, colorful
Opening, Moving, Waking
Sunrise, sunshine, shadows, sunset
Closing, slowing, sleeping
Dark, colorless
NIGHT

THE WAY WE WERE

WRITE ANECDOTES OR POEMS OR DIARY ENTRIES ABOUT YOUR YOUNGER DAYS. TELL ABOUT . . .

The worst thing that ever happened to me
The last time I sassed my mother
When Mr. Albertson tripped on my skateboard
The time my lizard got loose in Sunday School
My first day in kindergarten

SIX REASONS

WRITE SIX REASONS:

for tomatoes
why grades should be given
for going to school
why people eat
for having a pet
why I don't feel like writing
for eating vegetables
why friends have fights
for falling in love

REAL ESTATE AGENTS

BORROW SOME OLD HOUSE DESCRIPTIONS FROM A REALTOR. WATCH THE NEWSPAPERS TO SEE WHAT HOUSES ARE FOR SALE AND TO READ THE INFORMATION WRITTEN ABOUT THEM. WRITE UP DESCRIPTIONS OF SOME HOUSES FOR YOUR OWN FILE. (TRY YOUR OWN HOUSE AND YOUR NEIGHBOR'S OR FRIEND'S.) CAN YOU DO ONE ON YOUR SECRET CLUBHOUSE OR YOUR SCHOOL OR YOUR CLASSROOM OR A LOCAL STORE THAT WOULD CONVINCE SOMEONE TO SEE IT AS A GREAT BUY?

ENCYCLOPEDIA POEMS

CHOOSE SEVERAL INTERESTING FACTS FROM THE ENCYCLOPEDIA. USE ONE OR MORE OF THEM AS A LINE OR A THEME FOR A POEM. OR TURN THE WHOLE ENCYCLOPEDIA ENTRY INTO A RIDDLE OR POEM.

HORROR-SCOPES

IMAGINE AND WRITE HOROSCOPES FOR EACH OF THE ASTROLOGICAL SIGNS. MAKE THE HOROSCOPES SILLY OR UNUSUAL OR HORRIBLE. (THIS IS A GOOD IDEA FOR OCTOBER!)

YOU ARE UNDER MY SPELL

CAST A SPELL OR A HEX ON SOMEONE. TELL HOW AND WHY YOU DID IT. SEND THAT PERSON AN ANNOUNCEMENT THAT FILLS HER IN ON THE DETAILS OF HER FATE.

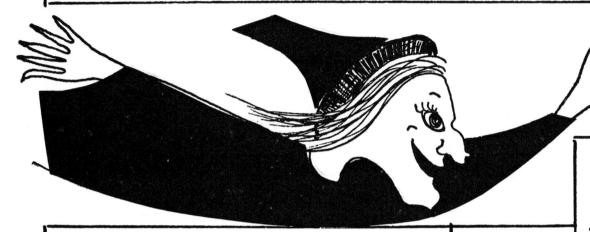

HOME REMEDIES

WRITE REMEDIES FOR . . . COMMON DISEASES . . . ILLNESSES . . . MINOR ACCIDENTS LIKELY TO HAPPEN AROUND THE HOME OR SCHOOL. THE CURES CAN BE SERIOUS OR SILLY . . .

How to get rid of freckles
What to do for a broken heart
How to live with a big nose
How to cure a sore throat or stuffy head
How to get rid of pinkeye

NEW NEWS FROM OLD TALES

TURN A FAIRY TALE OR ANY WELL-KNOWN STORY INTO A MODERN DAY NEWS STORY. GIVE IT A SENSATIONAL HEADLINE!

Woodcutter Saves Girl in Daring Rescue
Population Explosion Comes to Shoe-Town
Juvenile Attacked by Hungry Spider

MY LAST WILL AND TESTAMENT

AFTER READING SOME EXAMPLES OF REAL WILLS, WRITE (IN LEGAL LANGUAGE) WHAT YOU WISH TO LEAVE TO THE SCHOOL, THE TEACHER, OR THE NEW STUDENTS AS YOU LEAVE YOUR CLASS AND MOVE ON TO THE NEXT GRADE.

GHASTLY, GHOSTLY, GRUESOME TALES

SIT IN A CIRCLE WITH SOME FRIENDS AND COLLECT THE SCARIEST WORDS YOU CAN THINK OF. USE THE WORDS TO WRITE A VERY SPOOKY GHOST STORY. THEN GATHER IN A CIRCLE, TURN OUT THE LIGHTS AND TELL YOUR GHASTLY GOINGS-ON. IT'S OKAY TO HOLD SOMEONE'S HAND IF THE STORIES GET REALLY CREEPY!

People Watching ———————————→

WHERE?

SKI HILLS	CAR WASHES
STREETS	SWIMMING POOLS
PARKING LOTS	CAR DEALERS
STORES	MOVIES
TRAFFIC JAMS	SCHOOLS
BALL GAMES	CONCERTS
LIBRARIES	ON TELEVISION
HOMES	HOTELS
WEDDINGS	FUNERALS
BUS STATIONS	RESTAURANTS
MARKETS	PARTIES
IN LINES	IN OTHER CARS
THROUGH WINDOWS	BANKS
CARNIVALS	FAIRS
PARKS	ZOOS
JAILS	PLAYS
MUSEUMS	PHONE BOOTHS
TRAINS	BUSES
IN STROLLERS	HOSPITALS
OFFICES	PLAYGROUNDS
ELEVATORS	CHURCHES
BARBER SHOPS	SHOE STORES
ASSEMBLIES	DOCTORS' OFFICES

ANYWHERE . . . .

WHO?

PET OWNERS	PEOPLE:
PREACHERS	WORKING
SECRETARIES	MOPING
PILOTS	PLAYING
BIRDWATCHERS	SLEEPING
FRIENDS	THINKING
LOVERS	CRYING
TEACHERS	HELPING
ACTORS	HARMING
DRIVERS	LISTENING
ATHLETES	GIVING
NEIGHBORS	TAKING
MOTORCYCLISTS	FIGHTING
JOGGERS	EATING
STRANGERS	TALKING
ADULTS	HIKING
KIDS	RELAXING
TEENAGERS	HURTING
BABIES	SHARING
SHY PEOPLE	SMILING
TALL PEOPLE	SCOWLING
SHOW OFFS	WAITING
SKINNY PEOPLE	DOING NOTHING

ANYBODY . . .

HOW?

LOOK   AT A PERSON'S FACE . . . WHAT DOES IT TELL YOU ABOUT THE WAY SHE IS FEELING?
     WHAT HE'S THINKING?
     WHERE SHE'S GOING?
     WHAT HE'S LIKE?

NOTICE   FACIAL EXPRESSIONS
     BODY LANGUAGE (POSTURE, MOVEMENT, MANNERISMS)
     CLOTHING (TYPE, FIT, PURPOSE, COLOR)
     FRIENDLINESS (INTERACTION WITH OTHERS)

ASK
     YOURSELF   WHAT IS THIS PERSON DOING? IS IT WORK OR PLAY OR——————————?
     HOW DOES HE SEEM TO FEEL ABOUT WHAT HE IS DOING?
     DOES HE NOTICE OTHER PEOPLE? TALK TO OTHERS? IS SHE IN A WORLD BY HERSELF?
     HOW DOES SHE REACT TO THE OTHER PEOPLE OR SITUATIONS AROUND HER?
     WHAT DO YOU THINK YOU COULD LEARN FROM FOLLOWING OR WATCHING THIS PERSON?
     OF WHAT PLACES, SOUNDS, SONGS, COLORS, FEELINGS, IDEAS DOES THIS PERSON REMIND YOU? WHY?

ACTIVE PEOPLE-WATCHING

GET TO KNOW A PERSON THROUGH WATCHING,
THEN WRITE HIS/HER AUTOBIOGRAPHY.

FOR ONE PERSON THAT YOU'VE BEEN WATCHING, MAKE A VALUE LIST THAT TELLS THINGS YOU'VE
OBSERVED TO BE IMPORTANT TO THAT PERSON.

WATCH ONE PERSON. WHAT MIGHT THAT PERSON DO THAT WOULD GET PUT IN THE NEWSPAPER? WRITE
AN ARTICLE AS IT WOULD APPEAR IN THE PAPER.

INTERVIEW ONE OF THE PEOPLE YOU'VE WATCHED. FIND OUT:

How he/she describes his/her life and self . . .
What he/she likes . . . . . . and dislikes . . .
What she/he thinks is important or cares about . . .
What he/she wants to accomplish in life. . . .

ADD YOUR OWN FEELINGS AND OBSERVATIONS ABOUT THE PERSON. WRITE A SUMMARY OF THE INTER-
VIEW.

WRITE A JOURNAL ABOUT SOMEONE AFTER YOU'VE WATCHED F(
WHILE. DESCRIBE HIS/HER ACTIVITIES, BEHAVIOR, AND APPEARAN

WRITE A DIARY (FOR A WEEK) FOR A PERSON AS YOU THINK T
PERSON MIGHT WRITE IT.

DESIGN A BIRTHDAY CARD OR PERSONALIZED CALENDAR TO (
TO SOMEONE WHOM YOU'VE WATCHED.

PEOPLE ARE THE WORLD'S NUMBER ONE RESOURCE

CATCH THE PEOPLE-WATCHING FEVER! YOU CAN LEARN A LOT ABOUT HUMAN BEHAVIOR, INTERPER-SONAL RELATIONS, VALUES, OCCUPATIONS . . . AND FIND OUT ABOUT WHAT MAKES PEOPLE BE PEOPLE!

INVITE PEOPLE TO COME TO THE CLASSROOM SO THAT YOU CAN WATCH THEM DOING WHAT THEY LIKE TO DO.

Invite:
an artist to sculpt or paint or draw
a jeweler to repair a watch
a grandmother to crochet
a soda fountain operator to make a soda
an upholsterer to reupholster a chair
a dancer to rehearse
an electrician to repair an out-of-order socket
the school secretary to take a shorthand letter from the principal

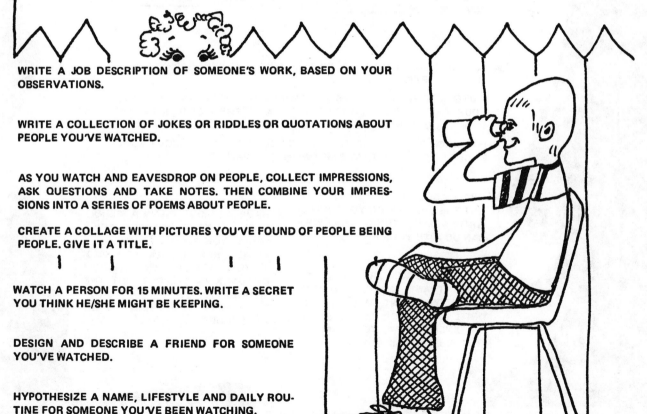

WRITE A JOB DESCRIPTION OF SOMEONE'S WORK, BASED ON YOUR OBSERVATIONS.

WRITE A COLLECTION OF JOKES OR RIDDLES OR QUOTATIONS ABOUT PEOPLE YOU'VE WATCHED.

AS YOU WATCH AND EAVESDROP ON PEOPLE, COLLECT IMPRESSIONS, ASK QUESTIONS AND TAKE NOTES. THEN COMBINE YOUR IMPRESSIONS INTO A SERIES OF POEMS ABOUT PEOPLE.

CREATE A COLLAGE WITH PICTURES YOU'VE FOUND OF PEOPLE BEING PEOPLE. GIVE IT A TITLE.

WATCH A PERSON FOR 15 MINUTES. WRITE A SECRET YOU THINK HE/SHE MIGHT BE KEEPING.

DESIGN AND DESCRIBE A FRIEND FOR SOMEONE YOU'VE WATCHED.

HYPOTHESIZE A NAME, LIFESTYLE AND DAILY ROUTINE FOR SOMEONE YOU'VE BEEN WATCHING.

"Me" Stuff

★ WRITE A POEM IN WHICH
EVERY OTHER LINE BEGINS:

I seem to be_____

But I really am_____

OR LIKE THIS:

I'm good at_____

I'm not so good at _____

★ FINISH THIS:

I am_____

I am_____

I am_____

I am_____

I am_____

★ FOR KIDS TOO YOUNG TO WRITE A FULL AUTOBIOGRAPHY, TRY A PICTO-BIOGRAPHY!

BRING IN SOME OLD PHOTOS AND RECENT PHOTOS OF YOURSELF AND YOUR FAMILY, PETS, FRIENDS, ETC. PASTE THE PICTURES IN ANY ORDER YOU WISH ON A LONG PIECE OF PAPER.

FOR EACH PICTURE, WRITE A SENTENCE THAT TELLS ABOUT SOME PIECE OF YOUR LIFE THAT'S SHOWN IN THAT PICTURE.

★ DRAW AROUND YOUR HAND. CUT OUT THE OUTLINE. ON YOUR HAND WRITE ALL THE THINGS THAT YOU CAN DO WITH YOUR HANDS.

★ HAVE SOMEONE DRAW A SILHOU-ETTE OF YOUR HEAD'S PROFILE WHILE YOU SIT IN FRONT OF A LIGHT FROM A FILMSTRIP PRO-JECTOR. "CATCH" THE SHADOW ON DARK PAPER. CUT OUT THE SILHOUETTE. PASTE WORDS ON IT THAT HAVE SOMETHING TO DO WITH YOURSELF.

★ DESIGN A FLAG FOR YOURSELF. MAKE IT ANY SHAPE, SIZE AND COLORS YOU WANT. ON THE FLAG, WRITE WORDS OR PHRASES OR SENTENCES THAT TELL ABOUT THINGS OR IDEAS IN WHICH YOU BELIEVE.

MAKE A ME-MOBILE BY HANGING FROM A HANGER PICTURES, WORDS, WRITING, AND OTHER THINGS THAT TELL OR SHOW ABOUT YOU. PUNCH A HOLE IN EACH ITEM AND SUSPEND IT FROM THE HANGER WITH STRING.

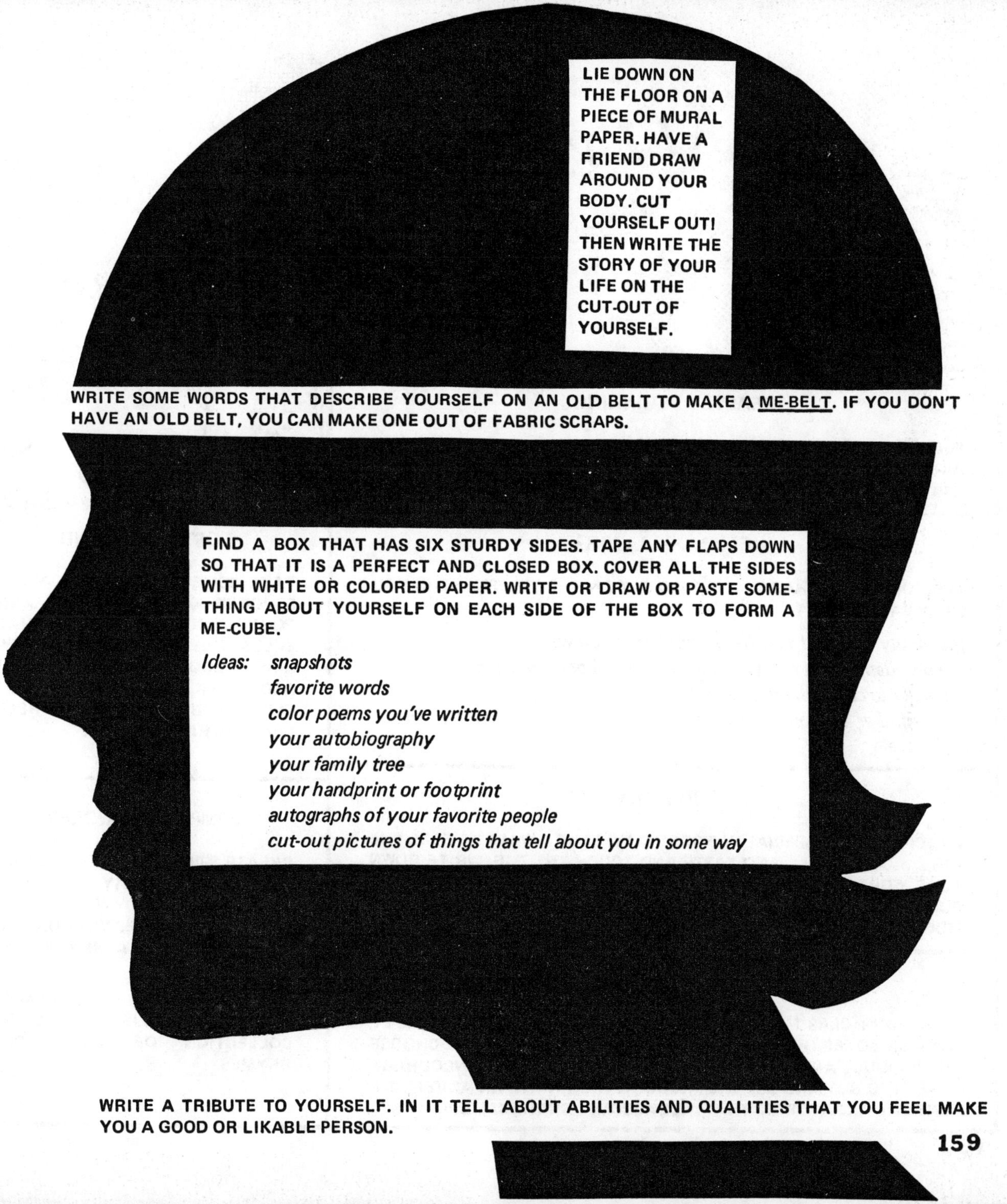

LIE DOWN ON THE FLOOR ON A PIECE OF MURAL PAPER. HAVE A FRIEND DRAW AROUND YOUR BODY. CUT YOURSELF OUT! THEN WRITE THE STORY OF YOUR LIFE ON THE CUT-OUT OF YOURSELF.

WRITE SOME WORDS THAT DESCRIBE YOURSELF ON AN OLD BELT TO MAKE A <u>ME-BELT</u>. IF YOU DON'T HAVE AN OLD BELT, YOU CAN MAKE ONE OUT OF FABRIC SCRAPS.

FIND A BOX THAT HAS SIX STURDY SIDES. TAPE ANY FLAPS DOWN SO THAT IT IS A PERFECT AND CLOSED BOX. COVER ALL THE SIDES WITH WHITE OR COLORED PAPER. WRITE OR DRAW OR PASTE SOMETHING ABOUT YOURSELF ON EACH SIDE OF THE BOX TO FORM A ME-CUBE.

Ideas: *snapshots*
favorite words
color poems you've written
your autobiography
your family tree
your handprint or footprint
autographs of your favorite people
cut-out pictures of things that tell about you in some way

WRITE A TRIBUTE TO YOURSELF. IN IT TELL ABOUT ABILITIES AND QUALITIES THAT YOU FEEL MAKE YOU A GOOD OR LIKABLE PERSON.

BEASTLY BEGINNINGS

IMAGINE, CREATE (WITH PAINT OR PAPER OR ANY OTHER MEDIUM) AND DESCRIBE (WITH WORDS) AN IMAGINARY CREATURE. TELL OR WRITE A STORY ABOUT ITS HABITS AND ADVENTURES.

HELLO, OPERATOR?

TELL OR WRITE WHAT YOU WOULD SAY ON THE TELEPHONE IF YOU WERE CALLING:

the library to find if they have a book that you want
the president to tell him your opinion on one of his policies
a theater to check the time of a movie
your mother at work to tell her about how the supper slid down the
   drain

FOG WALK

WATCH FOR AN ESPECIALLY FOGGY DAY. TAKE A WALK TO FEEL THE AIR . . . AND SMELL AND TASTE AND TOUCH THE FOG. WRITE DOWN SOME WORDS AND CAPTURE SOME PHRASES THAT CAN BE USED IN FOG POEMS. (TRY A WALK ON A RAINY OR SNOWY OR WINDY OR MUGGY DAY, TOO.)

SALES PITCH

WITH YOUR CLASSMATES, GATHER AND BRING TO SCHOOL EMPTY CANS OR BOXES OR BAGS FROM ALL SORTS OF PRODUCTS. CHOOSE ONE PRODUCT AND PREPARE A SALES PITCH THAT WILL ENCOURAGE OTHERS TO BUY AND USE THE PRODUCT. THEN WRITE AN ADVERTISE-MENT OR MAKE A POSTER THAT WILL ACCOMPLISH THE SAME PURPOSE.

LOST AND FOUND

TAKE SOMETHING OUT OF YOUR SCHOOL'S OR CLASS' LOST AND FOUND BOX. WRITE A CLUE THAT TELLS ONE THING YOU KNOW (FROM LOOKING AT THE ITEM) ABOUT ITS OWNER. READ YOUR CLUE TO THE CLASS; IT MAY HELP FIND THE RIGHT OWNER.

JUMP ROPE JINGLES

CREATE JINGLES AND STORIES AND RHYMES TO SAY WHILE YOU JUMP ROPE. START WITH A LINE THE TEACHER GIVES YOU—OR ADD A FEW LINES TO A RHYME YOU ALREADY KNOW.

JUMP THE ROPE JINGLES, BY EMMA WORSTELL (COLLIER) IS A GOOD COLLECTION OF JUMP ROPE RHYMES.

IT'S IN THE BAG!

CHOOSE ONE THING TO PUT INTO A SMALL PAPER BAG. STAPLE SHUT THE BAG. PASS IT AROUND TO YOUR CLASSMATES. ASK THEM TO WRITE WORDS ON THE BAG THAT TELL ABOUT THE ITEM (THEY CAN FEEL THROUGH THE BAG BUT MAY NOT OPEN IT). THEN, LET THEM OPEN THE BAG, AND WITH EYES CLOSED, FEEL AGAIN AND WRITE MORE WORDS.

STRETCHERS

TELL LIES AND STRETCHED STORIES ABOUT THINGS THAT COULD NEVER REALLY HAPPEN. THEN CUT A RUBBER BAND AND PRINT YOUR LIE ON IT. SEE HOW BIG THE LIE LOOKS WHEN IT'S STRETCHED OUT!

YOUNG GOURMETS

TELL SOMEONE HOW TO MAKE YOUR FAVORITE FOOD. ASK THAT PERSON TO WRITE DOWN THE RECIPE FOR YOU. A COLLECTION OF THESE FROM THE WHOLE CLASS MAKES A NICE PRESENT FOR MOTHER'S DAY!

BITS AND PIECES

FIND SOME PICTURES OF ANIMALS AND/OR PEOPLE. TRY TO CHOOSE PICTURES THAT ARE SIMILAR IN SIZE. CUT EACH ONE IN HALF AND MATCH A HALF WITH A DIFFERENT PICTURE TO FORM A NEW ANIMAL, PERSON OR CREATURE. THEN WRITE A STORY ABOUT THE NEW CREATURE.

A–B–C BOOKS

BRING LOTS OF ALPHABET BOOKS INTO YOUR ROOM. READ THEM ALL TO GET IDEAS ABOUT HOW THEY'RE WRITTEN. THEN, CHOOSE ONE LETTER OF THE ALPHABET (DECIDE ON THIS WITH THE REST OF THE GROUP, SO THAT ALL THE LETTERS GET CHOSEN). FOR THAT LETTER, WRITE SOME WORDS AND DRAW A PICTURE TO MAKE YOUR PAGE. THEN PUT IT TOGETHER WITH THE OTHER PAGES INTO YOUR CLASS A–B–C BOOK.

SUPER SNOOPERS

HIDE SOMETHING IN YOUR CLASSROOM. CHOOSE SOMETHING SMALL ENOUGH TO BE EASILY HIDDEN BUT LARGE ENOUGH TO BE FOUND. THEN WRITE CAREFUL DIRECTIONS FOR SOMEONE TO FOLLOW THAT WILL LEAD HIM OR HER TO THE TREASURE.

TASTING PARTY

BRING SAMPLES OF SOME TASTY THINGS. TRY TO GET A VARIETY OF DIFFERENT TASTES FOR YOUR GROUP. SET UP STATIONS WITH A DIFFERENT TASTING ITEM AT EACH. VISIT THE STATIONS, WRITING DOWN WORDS OR MAKING UP SIMILES FOR EACH TASTE. TRY A SMELLING PARTY TOO!

MIXED-UP-UP-MIXED FAIRY TALES

WRITE A NEW FAIRY TALE THAT IS MADE BY COMBINING PARTS OF FOUR OR FIVE OTHER FAIRY TALES. TRY THE SAME THING WITH NURSERY RHYMES.

HOW ABOUT A NEW ONE COMBINING:

The Ugly Duckling
Rumpelstiltskin
The Three Little Pigs
Hansel and Gretel

WHO AM I?

WRITE RIDDLES IN RHYME THAT GIVE PEOPLE CLUES ABOUT THE MYSTERY PERSON OR OBJECT.

You put me in a pig
You're glad if you have many.
Five of me makes a nickle
I'm a little copper _____ .

I've been called a flip-flop and a
*   sneak*
A tennie and loafer too.
I'm friendly with your foot.
I'm your good old favorite _____ .

FORTUNE TELLING

WRITE SOME FORTUNES FOR OTHER PEOPLE. THEN BAKE THEM INTO COOKIES. SHARE THE COOKIES WITH ONE ANOTHER. ANY KIND OF COOKIE WILL DO IF YOU FOLD THE FORTUNE UP REAL TINY— BUT IT'S FUN TO MAKE FORTUNE COOKIES—TRY THE REAL ONES!

STORY STEEPLES

COVER OLD BLOCKS WITH PAPER. WRITE WORDS OR PHRASES ON EACH SIDE OF EACH BLOCK. THEN YOU CAN BUILD DIFFERENT STORIES BY STACKING THE BLOCKS DIFFERENT WAYS.

TOUCH AND TELL SCRAPBOOKS

COLLECT SAMPLES OF THINGS THAT ARE INTERESTING TO TOUCH. PASTE EACH SAMPLE ON A PAGE IN A SCRAPBOOK. (YOU CAN MAKE YOUR OWN OR CONTRIBUTE TO ONE CLASS SCRAPBOOK.) ON EACH PAGE, WRITE SOME WORDS AND PHRASES THAT DESCRIBE THE TEXTURES AND THE FEELINGS.

Collecting ideas: *foil*   *sand paper*   *saw dust*
                        vinyl   *steel wool*   *dried glue*
                        plastic   *cotton*   *leaves*
                        cheese cloth *corduroy*

WORD HANG-UPS

HANG A PHOTOGRAPH OR MAGAZINE PICTURE FROM A HANGER. WRITE SOME WORDS OR PHRASES THAT DESCRIBE THE PICTURE. HANG THESE WITH THREAD FROM THE PICTURE. THEN TRY WRITING A SENTENCE USING SOME OF THE WORDS ON SOMEONE ELSE'S HANGER.

SAME SOUND SENTENCES

MAKE UP SENTENCES IN WHICH EVERY WORD BEGINS WITH THE SAME SOUND:

Debbie
dumped
damp
dirt
down
Dan's
daddy's
drain.

Such
strong
scents
started
Sally
sneezing.

ON THE AIR

PRETEND TO BE AN ANNOUNCER TELLING FLIGHT ARRIVALS AT AN AIRPORT OR ANNOUNCING A HALF-TIME SHOW AT A FOOTBALL GAME OR ACTING AS THE RINGMASTER AT A CIRCUS OR BROADCASTING A BASEBALL GAME ON THE RADIO OR TELLING THE WINNERS IN A CONTEST. GET READY TO TELL WHAT YOU WOULD BE SAYING IN THAT SITUATION.

POLAROID HISTORIES

IF YOUR TEACHER OR A CLASSMATE HAS AN INSTANT CAMERA, HAVE SOMEONE TAKE PICTURES OF ACTIVITIES GOING ON IN YOUR CLASSROOM THROUGH THE YEAR. USE THE PHOTOS AS ILLUSTRATIONS FOR A CLASS "HISTORY OF THIS SCHOOL YEAR." FOR EACH PICTURE, WRITE SENTENCES TO TELL ABOUT WHAT WAS HAPPENING. IN THIS WAY YOU CAN BUILD A PICTORIAL HISTORY TOGETHER.

INTERVIEWS

HELP YOUR GROUP CHOOSE A PERSON ABOUT WHOM YOU'D LIKE TO KNOW MORE. IT MIGHT BE A LOCAL SHOE REPAIR PERSON OR THE PRINCIPAL OR A FIFTH GRADER OR THE SCHOOL COOK OR THE MAN WHO DELIVERS PAPER CUPS TO THE CAFETERIA . . . OR ANYBODY. CONTRIBUTE ONE QUESTION TO A LIST OF THINGS PEOPLE WOULD LIKE TO FIND OUT. THEN SELECT A REPRESENTATIVE OR TWO FROM THE GROUP TO DO THE INTERVIEW AND REPORT THE RESULTS.

STORIES IN THE ROUND

SIT IN A CIRCLE. HAVE SOMEONE START A STORY WITH ONE SENTENCE. PASS THE STORY AROUND THE CIRCLE. EACH PERSON SHOULD ADD ONE SENTENCE. IF THE STORY FINISHES BEFORE THE CIRCLE FINISHES, START A NEW STORY!

CLOTHESLINE TALES

CUT OUT FROM CONSTRUCTION PAPER SHAPES THAT LOOK LIKE DIFFERENT ARTICLES OF CLOTHING. ON EACH ONE, WRITE A WORD OR PHRASE (OR THE TEACHER CAN DO THIS FOR YOU). THEN USE CLOTHESPINS TO HANG THE CLOTHING IN AN ORDER THAT WILL FORM A SENTENCE. YOU CAN REARRANGE THE WORDS DIFFERENTLY TO MAKE NEW SENTENCES.

ESPECIALLY, BUT NOT ONLY,

FOR *RELUCTANT* WRITERS

PASS IT ON

SIT IN A CIRCLE WITH YOUR CLASS. WHEN THE TEACHER OR LEADER SAYS, "START," WRITE A GOOD BEGINNING FOR A STORY. WHEN THE TEACHER SAYS, "TRADE," PASS YOUR PAPER DOWN TWO PEOPLE. THEN, READ THE PAPER YOU'VE RECEIVED AND WRITE A GOOD MIDDLE. WHEN THE TEACHER SAYS, "PASS," SEND YOUR STORY ON AGAIN. THIS TIME ADD A STRONG, EXCITING ENDING TO THE STORY YOU RECEIVE. WHEN IT'S TIME TO PASS AGAIN, ADD A TITLE TO THE NEW STORY THAT YOU GET. THEN SHARE THE FINAL STORIES WITH EACH OTHER. (YOU MIGHT WANT TO DECIDE AHEAD OF TIME WITH THE GROUP ON A THEME FOR THE STORIES.)

REVISED COPY

REWRITE NURSERY RHYMES TO MAKE THEM CONTEMPORARY OR RE-WRITE A STORY YOU HAVE READ SO THAT IT'S WRITTEN IN LANGUAGE FOR YOUNGER CHILDREN.

YOU'RE NUTS!

CRACK OPEN A WALNUT CAREFULLY SO YOU DON'T BREAK EITHER HALF. THEN WRITE AN IDEA FOR A NUTTY WRITING STARTER (A JOKE OR RIDDLE OR SILLY TALE) AND PUT IT IN THE NUT SHELL. GLUE THE SHELL HALVES BACK TOGETHER. HANG THE NUT ON A DEAD TREE BRANCH SO SOMEONE ELSE CAN PICK IT AND USE IT AS A BEGINNING.

Samples:
The tooth fairy
that gets sick
at the sight of
teeth . . .
A rock band
made up of
singing bananas . .
A flea with a
pet giant . . .
A typewriter
that's taking
over the world . .

10 THINGS

MAKE A LIST OF ANY OF THE IDEAS BELOW (OR ADD YOUR OWN IDEA). LIST 10 THINGS:

. . . to do last
. . . to do first
. . . never to do
. . . I don't understand
. . . that should be changed
. . . to keep secret
. . . to do before breakfast
. . . I'll never forget
. . . I'd like to forget
. . . I'll never regret
. . . about my city
. . . about teeth
. . . never to tell your mother
. . . to do slowly
. . . to do in a hurry
. . . you should try
. . . to say to a gorilla
. . . to tell your teacher if you didn't
  do your homework
. . . that make me mad

MAKE A LIST OF TEN THINGS TO WHICH YOU WOULD SAY "YES!"

CAPTIONED!

COLLECT CARTOONS AND INTERESTING PICTURES. CUT OFF THE WRITING THAT'S UNDER THE PICTURES. TRADE CARTOONS WITH FRIENDS (OR KEEP YOUR OWN) AND WRITE NEW CAPTIONS FOR THEM.

MAKE A LIST OF TEN THINGS TO WHICH YOU WOULD SAY "NO!"

TELEGRAMS

TELEGRAMS ARE LIMITED TO 15 WORDS. THEY USUALLY LEAVE OUT SMALL, UNNECESSARY WORDS. WRITE AN URGENT MESSAGE OR TELL ABOUT SOMETHING IMPORTANT THAT'S HAPPENED—IN A TELEGRAM. REMEMBER, ONLY 15 WORDS ALLOWED!

WOULD YOU BELIEVE?

TELL OR WRITE LIES—REALLY BIG WHOPPERS — ABOUT THE WEATHER, FISHING TRIPS, EATING, ANIMALS, PEOPLE, ANYTHING!

It was so hot that _____
He was so fast that _____
Yesterday was colder than _____
The fish was as big as _____

PHOETRY

PHOETRY IS A COMBINATION OF POETRY AND PHOTOGRAPHY. TAKE (OR BRING IN) SNAPSHOTS OF ANYTHING THAT INTERESTS YOU. THEN WRITE POETRY TO DESCRIBE ACTIONS, IMPRESSIONS, FEELINGS OR PLACES REPRESENTED IN THE PICTURES.

SECRETS

WRITE SECRET MESSAGES WITH INVISIBLE INK (LEMON JUICE OR VINEGAR OR APPLE JUICE). DO THE WRITING WITH A SMALL BRUSH OR A Q-TIP OR YOUR FINGER. THEN PASS THE SECRETS TO A FRIEND. YOUR FRIEND CAN DECIPHER THE WORDS BY HOLDING THE PAPER CLOSE TO A HOT LIGHT. THE WRITING WILL TURN BROWN.

CROSSWORDS BACKWARDS

GIVE STUDENTS A CROSSWORD PUZZLE FILLED IN. ASK THEM TO MAKE UP THE CLUES FOR EACH WORD.

WORD BOWL

FILL A BOWL (OR AN OLD HAT) WITH INTERESTING WORDS. THEN PASS THE BOWL SO THAT EACH STUDENT CAN CHOOSE ONE (OR TWO OR THREE) WITHOUT LOOKING. USE YOUR WORDS AS STARTERS FOR A JOKE OR STORY OR POEM. OR, USE THEM IN A TITLE. YOU MIGHT WANT TO COMBINE WORDS WITH A FRIEND AND WORK TOGETHER. SOMETIMES IT'S FUN TO WORK AS A WHOLE CLASS AND TRY TO USE ALL THE WORDS CHOSEN IN ONE STORY.

TRANSLATIONS

FIND A POEM THAT'S WRITTEN IN A FOREIGN LANGUAGE. "TRANSLATE" IT BY WRITING WHAT YOU THINK THE POEM SAYS.

SCHNEEFLÖCKCHEN, WEIBRÖCKCHEN,
   WANN KOMMST DU GESCHNEIT?
DU WOHNST IN DER WOLKE,
   DEIN WEG IST SO WEIT.
KOMM, SETZ DITCH ANS FENSTER,
   DU LIEBLICHER STERN,
   MALST BLUMEN UND BLÄTTER.
WIR HABEN DICH GERN.

Sally, Willy,
   want to come to school?
You stay on the walk
   or your feet are so wet.
Don't set the desk on fire,
   the teacher is mean,
   mostly he yells and blabbers
When you have your desk gone.

RAMBLING-MIND WRITING

WHEN YOU'RE HAVING A HARD TIME CONCENTRATING ON ONE IDEA, WRITE IN A STREAM-OF-CONSCIOUSNESS STYLE. THAT MEANS: LET YOUR PENCIL FOLLOW YOUR MIND! JUST WRITE ABOUT ANYTHING AND EVERYTHING THAT COMES INTO YOUR MIND—EVEN IF THE IDEAS ARE NOT RELATED TO EACH OTHER. LATER, YOU MIGHT PICK OUT ONE OF THOSE IDEAS AND CONCENTRATE ON IT FOR WRITING SOMETHING.

UNDER INSPECTION

THE NEXT TIME YOU GO TO A RESTAURANT

OR AN OFFICE
OR A SHOE STORE
OR A BALL GAME . . .

PRETEND YOU ARE AN OFFICIAL INSPECTOR.

TAKE NOTES ON THE QUALITY OF THE FOOD OR OTHER GOODS. NOTICE THE SERVICE, THE CLEANLINESS, THE SAFETY.

WRITE A RESUME OF YOUR FINDINGS. IF YOU'RE BRAVE ENOUGH, SHARE YOUR REPORT WITH THE ESTABLISHMENT.

ESPECIALLY, BUT NOT ONLY,

FOR *GIFTED*

WRITERS

INTERVIEWS

WRITE AT LEAST TEN QUESTIONS IN PREPARATION FOR INTERVIEWING SOMEONE. YOU CAN CHOOSE ANYONE FROM A KINDERGARTNER TO A TAXI DRIVER. WHEN YOU'VE DONE THE INTERVIEW, WRITE IT UP IN DIALOGUE FORM.

HOW IS A DUCK LIKE A STOMACH ACHE?

SEE IF YOU CAN MAKE SOME UNUSUAL COMPARISONS LIKE THESE. FOR EACH ONE BE READY TO EXPLAIN WHY YOU ARE COMPARING THE TWO THINGS (WHAT THEY HAVE IN COMMON).

*Fresh air and potato chips are alike because*_____

*A goldfish is as*_____ *as a math test because* _____

Losing a friend is as _____ *as riding on a ferris wheel.*

*I am like*_____ *(a food)* _____ *because* _____

MONOLOGUES

MONOLOGUES ARE GRAND SPEECHES THAT YOU MAKE TO THE WORLD OR TO SOMEONE IN PARTICULAR FROM THE SAFE POSITION OF BEING ABSOLUTELY ALONE WITH NO ONE TO HEAR.

TRY WRITING A MONOLOGUE THAT MIGHT EXPRESS THE THOUGHTS OF A FAMOUS PERSON IN ANY SITUATION YOU CHOOSE—FROM THE PRESENT OR THE PAST.

HIDE-A-WORD

PASS OUT A WORD TO EACH STUDENT. LABEL IT "TOP SECRET." THE TASK IS TO WRITE A PARAGRAPH OR STORY IN WHICH THE WORD IS HIDDEN. (DON'T SPLIT UP THE WORD—USE IT WHOLE.) THE IDEA IS TO MAKE THAT WORD AS INCONSPICUOUS AS POSSIBLE. AFTER THEY'VE WRITTEN THE STORIES, STUDENTS CAN READ THEM ALOUD WHILE OTHERS TRY TO GUESS WHICH WORD WAS THE ONE THEY WERE TRYING TO HIDE.

FORTUNE-TELLING

ASK SEVERAL "CLIENTS" (INCLUDING YOURSELF AND THE TEACHER) TO CONTRIBUTE DESCRIPTIONS OF THEMSELVES, THEIR LIKES AND THEIR DISLIKES. THEN CHOOSE ONE OF THE DESCRIPTIONS AND ACT AS A FORTUNE TELLER. REPLY TO THE PERSON WITH PREDICTIONS AS TO WHAT YOU SEE HAPPENING IN HIS OR HER FUTURE. TRY TO SOLICIT SOME CLIENTS FROM OUTSIDE YOUR CLASS TOO!

METAMORPHOSIS

YOU WAKE UP IN THE MORNING OR YOU COME TO AFTER A STORM, AND YOU FIND YOU ARE SOMETHING OR SOMEWHERE DIFFERENT. WRITE ABOUT THE CHANGE. TELL WHAT HAS HAPPENED AND WHAT YOU HAVE BECOME.

RE-WRITE A WELL-KNOWN STORY FROM THE VIEWPOINT OF A DIFFERENT CHARACTER THAN THE ONE WHO IS THE "STAR" IN THE ORIGINAL VERSION.

For example: Tell about Red Riding Hood's experience from the wolf's viewpoint.

OR *describe Thanksgiving Dinner from the point of view of the turkey.*

OR *Tell about the whale's encounter with Jonah.*

OR *Re-tell the story of JAWS from the shark's view.*

SYNESTHESIA

THINK ABOUT THINGS THAT ARE USUALLY PERCEIVED BY ONE SENSE (SIGHT, HEARING, ETC.) AS THEY WOULD SEEM WHEN PERCEIVED THROUGH ONE OF THE OTHER SENSES. WRITE A DESCRIPTION OF:

how yellow might smell . . . or a sandwich might sound . . . or how a plan tastes . . . or what noise feels like . . . or how pain looks . . . or . . .

POETRY, POETRY, HERE, THERE, EVERYWHERE!

START WITH A NEWS ARTICLE OR AN ADVERTISEMENT OR THE LABEL ON A BOX OR AN ARGUMENT OR A STORY . . . AND TURN IT INTO A POEM. USE THE SAME INFORMATION AND IDEAS, BUT WRITE THEM IN A POETIC FORM.

QUOTATIONS BARTLETT NEVER HEARD

COLLECT INTERESTING QUOTES FROM ALL KINDS OF SOURCES . . . BOOKS YOU'VE READ, CLASSMATES, FRIENDS, PEOPLE ON THE STREET, TV PROGRAMS, FOLKS IN YOUR SCHOOL . . . TRY TO INCLUDE MANY KINDS OF QUOTES FROM MANY KINDS OF PEOPLE. ADD YOUR OWN QUOTES AND PRINT UP YOUR COLLECTION NEATLY INTO A BOOKLET.

YELLOW YELLOW PAGES

MAKE A DIRECTORY OF ALL THE GOODS AND SERVICES AVAILABLE WITHIN YOUR SCHOOL OR CLASSROOM. WRITE AN ADVERTISEMENT FOR EACH OF THE OFFERINGS AND ALPHABETICAL ENTRIES FOR ALL OF THEM. COMPILE THESE INTO YOUR OWN YELLOW PAGES. PRINT THEM UP ON YELLOW (OF COURSE) PAPER. SEE THE PHONE BOOK'S YELLOW PAGES FOR A SAMPLE.

WHAT A JOB!

START BY MAKING A LIST OF JOBS THAT SEEM AS IF THEY'D BE INTERESTING. INCLUDE SOME OF THE JOBS FROM YOUR CLASSROOM TOO.

THEN, MAKE AN APPLICATION BLANK FOR ONE OF THE JOBS TO BE FILLED OUT BY PROSPECTIVE EMPLOYEES. ALSO, WRITE A JOB DESCRIPTION TELLING WHAT KINDS OF WORK WOULD BE EXPECTED OF THAT EMPLOYEE.

CHOOSE ONE OF THE JOBS FOR WHICH YOU WOULD LIKE TO APPLY. WRITE A RESUME OF YOURSELF TELLING ABOUT YOUR EXPERIENCES AND YOUR PERSONAL QUALITIES THAT WOULD QUALIFY YOU FOR THE JOB.

IDEAS FOR MIXING WRITING WITH OTHER CONTENT AREAS

> Look for writing opportunities in every other discipline or activity. After all, poetry and prose are made of life's experiences; so history, geometry, language, physical activity, photography, social interaction and all other areas of study stir impressions and responses that can be expressed in words.

- **CHANTS** with sand paintings
- **MYSTERIES** with a shadow show
- **BIBLIOGRAPHIES** with portraits
- **VALUE STATEMENTS** with totem poles
- **EPITAPHS** with crayon grave rubbings
- **SPOOKY TALES** with black crayon resists
- **SNOW POETRY** with soap bubble paintings
- **COLOR WORDS OR PHRASES** with tie dyeing
- **MONSTER TALES** with squished paint blobs
- **CHARACTER SKETCHES** with cartoon sketches
- **WIND POEMS** with pinwheels or wind chimes
- **HAIKU** with silkscreens or bamboo painting
- **PICTURESQUE PHRASES** with torn paper scenes
- **EARTH POETRY** with rock painting or mud painting
- **DESCRIPTIONS OF SCENES** with wet watercolor paintings
- **LIES or TALL TALES** with oversized, exaggerated creatures
- **LIMERICKS** with crazy gourd characters or vegetable people
- **CITY POEMS or OBSERVATIONS ON CITY LIFE** with skyline paintings
- **ECOLOGY POSTERS or ECOLOGICAL BUMPERSTICKERS** with junk sculpture
- **IMPRESSIONISTIC POETRY** with paper mosaics or crayoned pointilism
- **POEMS ABOUT FEELINGS** with melted crayon or smeared chalk designs
- **PRAYERS or PROVERBS** with clay plaques or word collages or stained glass designs
- **POEMS or TALES ABOUT FACES AND THE PEOPLE BEHIND THEM** with paper mache masks
- **AUTOBIOGRAPHIES or ME-POEMS** with body outlines or face silhouettes or personal collages

- Plan a NEW BUSINESS or develop a NEW PRODUCT or offer a NEW SERVICE . . . . . . then . . .

design packaging	create advertisements
write contracts	form job descriptions for employees
write jingles	make lists of prospective customers
make up slogans	write a resume of your services
design a catalog	invent a business name and logo

- Write BIRTH CERTIFICATES for yourself or famous persons.

- Write ANNOUNCEMENTS for events that happened in the past.

- Write ROLE AUTOBIOGRAPHIES . . . describing your behavior and the expectations for your actions in one of your roles as a member of a group.

- Compile a SCRAPBOOK OF FAMILY HISTORY, including a family tree and interesting information about your past. Write letters to relatives to get information.

- Make a TIME LINE showing the major events and influences in your life.

- Keep a VALUES NOTEBOOK—composed of pictures that represent values which you hold. For each picture, write an explanation of how that picture shows that value. Find some pictures that depict others' values, too.

- Put together a PHOTO and WORD essay on current key figures in the world today.

- Write a GOSSIP COLUMN about celebrities as it might have appeared in a newspaper at a specific time in the past.

- Write TRAVEL BROCHURES . . . for any place . . . here or there . . . now or in the past.

- Turn a current event into a TALL TALE.

- Paint a WORD PORTRAIT OF A FRIENDSHIP. To gather ideas, ask people of all ages and kinds to tell you about their friends.

- Develop a FLAG, SEAL, SYMBOL, PLEDGE or NATIONAL ANTHEM for a new country.

- Write a TRIBUTE to the Red Cross or any other organization that serves people in the world today or in the past.

- Write a PROTECT-YOUR-ENVIRONMENT HANDBOOK for children, telling ways that young people can contribute to the preservation of resources.

SOCIAL STUDIES

- Write DIRECTIONS for an original math game that will help players learn math facts.

- Make up JUMP-ROPE RHYMES using the multiplication facts.

- Write a SPEECH that will convince someone to love math.

- Write imaginative WORD PROBLEMS for other people to solve. Use the names of your classmates in the problems.

- Write a LOVE STORY about a romance between a circle and a trapezoid.

- Write a POEM using at least ten math words.

- Write a PLAY about the "Wonderful World of Zero."

- Write the AUTOBIOGRAPHY of a right angle.

- Write a DIET for an overweight ton.

- Write up a CONTRACT between yourself and someone who is buying your bike on time payments.

- Write a MENU for a restaurant where a family of four could eat dinner for under $12.00.

- Write COUPLETS that will help you remember your addition facts.

- Make a NO NUMBER booklet telling what the world would be like without numbers.

- Write a SONG that explains how division works.

- Compile your own MATH DICTIONARY that has clear definitions of the math terms you use.

- Write an ODE to the number 17 (or any other) telling why that number is special.

- Make SIGNS, POSTERS and ADVERTISING BILLBOARDS telling about the discounts that will be available at an upcoming sale.

- Make a DIRECTORY of METRIC MEASURES. Explain the metric system so that your directory could be used by someone who hasn't yet learned metrics.

- Write DIRECTIONS telling how to make a cube or any other geometric figure.

- Write a BOOK JACKET for your math book . . . or an INDEX . . . or TABLE OF CONTENTS . . . or write a REVIEW of the book.

- Write ADVERTISING FOLDERS for resorts, camps, cruises, hotels. Figure out what your rates will be for individuals, families and groups.

- Make a RECIPE and MENU BOOK giving menus for well-balanced meals for a family.
- Write the LIFE STORY of a jellyfish or tadpole.
- Write a SCHEDULE for the care and feeding of the classroom pet (or your pet at home).
- Make a DIRECTORY of common diseases. Describe symptoms and cures for each.
- Write a RESUME of your qualifications to be class zoo-keeper or plant-tender.
- Write a TRIBUTE to your teeth or hair or vocal chords or muscles.
- Write DIRECTIONS for making a bug-catcher or for preserving animal tracks.
- Write a TONGUE TWISTER about tongues or tendons.
- After growing crystals, create CRYSTAL-SHAPED poems.
- Prepare a CONSUMER'S GUIDE of 50 ways to conserve water.
- When you're studying the universe, write SPACE FANTASIES.
- Write SUPERSTITIONS. Then explain scientifically why they can't be true.
- Write an INDEX or TABLE OF CONTENTS for a book on earthquakes or engines or seasons or electricity.

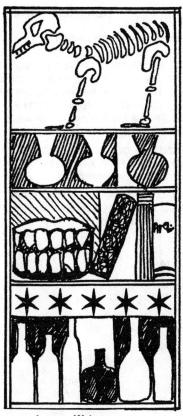

- Keep DATA SHEETS . . . careful records and notes on any science experiment. Write an hypothesis before you begin and a summary when you finish.
- Write WEATHER MYTHS to explain weather conditions or any other phenomena that persons long ago might not have understood.
- Create a SCIENCE CALENDAR. On each month's page, write and illustrate interesting scientific facts and discoveries.
- Compile a booklet of FIRST AID PROCEDURES for a school, a home or a camping trip.
- Write WEATHER POEMS or PERSONIFICATION STORIES about clouds or hailstones or tornadoes.
- Write a FAMILY ALBUM of your own ROOTS . . . describe the traits you inherited.
- Write QUESTIONS for INTERVIEWING a geologist, etymologist, microbiologist, chemist, hematologist, meterologist, pharmacist, icthyologist or physicist.
- Make a DIRECTORY of plants, land forms, birds, arachnids or reptiles. Draw 15 or more of each, label and write distinguishing characteristics.

SCIENCE

WEATHERGRAMS

A WEATHERGRAM IS A VERY SHORT POEM (10 WORDS OR LESS) THAT IS NOT FINISHED WHEN YOU FINISH IT. IT GETS FINISHED BY THE WEATHER! IT IS WRITTEN IN PERMANENT INK (WITH BEAUTIFUL HANDWRITING) ON A 2½ BY 10 INCH PIECE OF PAPER CUT FROM A BROWN GROCERY BAG. AFTER YOU'VE WRITTEN IT, YOU FOLD THE TOP, PUNCH A HOLE AND THREAD IT WITH A PIECE OF TWINE. THEN YOU HANG THE POEM ON A BUSH OR BRANCH IN YOUR YARD, IN THE WOODS OR ALONG A TRAIL.

AS IT HANGS OUT OF DOORS, IT IS FINISHED BY THE SNOW AND WIND AND SUN AND RAIN. AFTER ABOUT THREE MONTHS OF WEATHERING, IT BECOMES A TRUE WEATHERGRAM.

WRITE ABOUT SOMETHING THAT HAS TO DO WITH NATURE OR THE SEASONS. HANG IT IN A PLACE WHERE PASSERS-BY CAN ENJOY AND PONDER YOUR BRIEF THOUGHT. DO NOT SIGN YOUR NAME. JUST MAKE A SMALL SYMBOL OR INITIAL TO MARK IT AS YOURS.

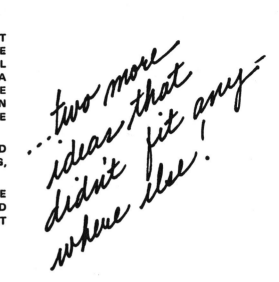

...two more ideas that didn't fit any where else!

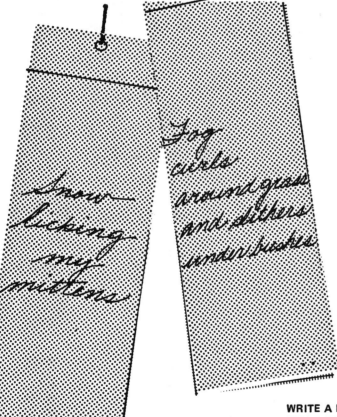

Snow licking my mittens

Fog circles around grass and slithers under bushes

ALPHABETICALLY SPEAKING

B was born with a bang!
It's Bewitching
  Brainy
  and Beautiful!
B has a Billion in the Bank
And Believes in the Bible.
It has seen a Bazooka
  in the Bayou
And a Bawdy Bartender
  on a Balcony.
B Buzzes, Bops, Bites, and Blabbers.
And it Beguiles,
  Bedazzles and Bewilders.
It's Been a Bachelor and a Bigamist.
B is always on its Best Behavior
Except when it Blunders
  Into Bootlegging.

Marguerite & Leon Grade 5

WRITE A POEM THAT SHOWS OFF ONE LETTER OF THE ALPHABET! (OR TRY A POEM IN WHICH EACH LINE CONCENTRATES ON A DIFFERENT LETTER.) CAN YOU DO THE WHOLE ALPHABET?

9 RESOURCES

"Help!"

Not All The Good Ideas Are Found In Books!

**Philosophy, Techniques, Inspiration And
Encouragement For Teachers**

Just Dozens and Dozens Of Ideas

**Special Books For Stimulating Writing And
Spreading Love of Language**

Favorite Collections Of Poetry

Record some of your favorite resources in this space!

NOT ALL THE GOOD IDEAS ARE FOUND IN BOOKS

This chapter offers and describes to you the BOOKS that are my most used and prized sources of inspiration and ideas. I hope you'll use and love them! However, as you do, be aware that hundreds of good writing sessions begin in classrooms each day without the aid of idea books. The treasures found in these references will open doors to expression for your kids. Please keep your door open to invite in the winds which carry other seeds for writing!

People are great idea sources. Watch and listen to:

your kids	other kids
parents	visitors
strangers	other teachers

Sometimes beginnings are suggested by your surroundings. Pay special attention to: sounds, sights, smells, textures

issues, problems, tragedies, questions, absurdities

human dilemmas, human achievements

As your senses sharpen, and as sensitivity to the environment increases for your students, all of you will begin to think of worlds of topics and reasons for writing.

Talk about yourselves	your discoveries
your feelings	your dreams
your experiences	your fantasies

For, out of your listening and talking and watching, new possibilities will abound so generously that you'll never be able to write about them all!

PHILOSOPHY, TECHNIQUES, INSPIRATION AND ENCOURAGEMENT FOR TEACHERS

Anderson, Douglas. MY SISTER LOOKS LIKE A PEAR: AWAKENING THE POETRY IN YOUNG PEOPLE. Hart, 1974.

Concrete advice for awakening creativity in children PLUS many examples of student writing gathered from the author's experiences writing with 15,000 kids in the Poets In The Schools Program.

Arnstein, Flora. POETRY AND THE CHILD. Dover, 1962.

Reasons and means for making poetry a living force in children's development. It is also a good source of student writing.

Hopkins, Lee Bennett. PASS THE POETRY, PLEASE! Citation Press, 1972.

A very thorough treatment of the values of and techniques for bringing poetry and children together. Covering everything from Mother Goose to LeRoi Jones, this is a rich resource of poems and suggested sources of poems for all purposes, and it's full of ideas for stimulating writing experiences in your classroom.

176

Koch, Kenneth. ROSE, WHERE DID YOU GET THAT RED? Vintage, 1973.

A believer in teaching the "great" poems to kids of all ages, Koch outlines ten lessons, each using a poem by Blake, Donne, Shakespeare or other well-known poet. Then he supplies an anthology of poems to use with kids, including brief teaching ideas for each. Try these with any age, but specifically with your older or gifted writers.

————. WISHES, LIES AND DREAMS. Vintage, 1970.

A poet relates his poetry-writing experiences with kids and crams the book with samples of writing by kids of all ages. A great source of student examples for motivating your writers.

Larrick, Nancy, ed. SOMEBODY TURNED ON A TAP IN THESE KIDS. Dell, 1971.

An inspiring collection of practical essays by writers who've spent hours writing with students. For an uplift and for dozens of ideas and hints from people who are really doing it, this is heartily recommended.

Lusk, Daniel. HOMEMADE POEMS. Lame Johnny Press, 1974.

Anyone can make poems! Good ideas . . . lots of original writing . . . many sensitive, helpful thoughts on writing with kids. This is the book that inspired me to start "preaching" poetry to teachers!

Mearns, Hughes. CREATIVE POWER: EDUCATION OF YOUTH IN THE CREATIVE ARTS. Dover, 1958.

A powerful and serious look at the education of children in art, drama, writing. The author shares personal experiences of writing with kids and a wealth of thoughts on how to stimulate the creative processes.

Painter, Helen. POETRY AND CHILDREN. International Reading Association, 1970.

Suggestions for guiding children to enjoyment of poetry and a good selection of poems right for sharing with children.

Petty, Walter and Mary Bowen. SLITHERY SNAKES AND OTHER AIDS TO CHILDREN'S WRITING. Appleton-Century-Crofts, 1967.

An old favorite! It is an easy-to-use paperback containing the how and when and where and why of creative writing plus dozens of specific ideas.

Staudacher, Carol. CREATIVE WRITING IN THE CLASSROOM. Fearon, 1968.

Rules and methods for creating the writing climate and for guiding the writing of descriptions, stories and poems. It includes some good ideas for specific lessons and a nice selection of children's original writing.

Whitman, Ruth and Harriet Feinberg. POEMMAKING. Massachusetts Council of Teachers of English, 1975.

Heartwarming and practical . . . a collection of fifteen accounts by poets of their experiences making poems with teachers and kids. It is filled with ideas, suggestions, personal feelings and successes and failures in the writing process—AND a wonderful sampling of kids' writing.

JUST DOZENS AND DOZENS OF IDEAS

Bogojavlensky, Ann, *et al.*   THE GREAT LEARNING BOOK.   Addison-Wesley, 1977.

A resource book that suggests ways of bringing the whole real world into the classroom, and in doing so, provides endless possibilities for writing experiences. It describes books related to numerous topics and provides excerpts from the books—so, in itself it is an idea book.

Brown, Rosellen, *et al.*   THE WHOLE WORD CATALOG.   Teachers' and Writers' Collaborative, 1972.

One of the best collections of writing ideas and directions for all levels. An interesting assortment of catalysts with kid-appeal.

Cataldo, John.   WORDS AND CALLIGRAPHY FOR CHILDREN.   Reinhold, 1969.

A beautiful and unusual book—illustrated in vivid color by children—of great ideas concerning the art in words. The artwork is often accompanied by or intertwined with writing.

Forte, Imogene, *et al.*   CORNERING CREATIVE WRITING.   Incentive, 1974.

Learning centers, games and activities designed to set the stage for and encourage imaginative writing and writing skills.

————.   KIDS' STUFF READING AND LANGUAGE EXPERIENCES, INTERMEDIATE/JR. HIGH.   Incentive, 1973.

Ideas for all the language arts for grades 4-9. It contains a hearty section on creative writing and writing skills.

Forte, Imogene and Joy MacKenzie.   KIDS' STUFF READING AND LANGUAGE EXPERIENCES, PRIMARY.   Incentive, 1974.

A language arts idea book for teachers which includes a large section of suggestions on writing for grades 1-4.

Grimm, Gary and Don Mitchell.   THE CEMETERY BOX.   Good Apple, 1976.

A creative kit of student-ready durable cards—each with an imaginative activity or stimulator to creative thinking and writing—ALL motivated by the natural fascination with the spooks and creatures and legends of cemeteries.

————.   THE GOOD APPLE CREATIVE WRITING BOOK.   Good Apple, 1976.

For all grade levels, a fun and practical but seriously skill-oriented group of usable ideas for working with words, phrases, stories, poems, letters and other forms of writing. Includes ideas for centers and some sensible talk about the writing climate.

Kaplan, Sandra, *et al.*   THE BIG BOOK OF WRITING GAMES AND ACTIVITIES.   Goodyear, 1975.

Several ready-made, brightly-colored and laminated centers to punch out and put together for students to use on their own. Teacher directions and student worksheets are included.

————.   A YOUNG CHILD EXPERIENCES.   Goodyear, 1975.

One of the best idea books I've found that's written specifically for very young children. It includes several pre-writing and language appreciation activities.

King, Joyce and Carol Katzman. IMAGINE THAT! Goodyear, 1976.

Illustrated poems and creative exercises set to ignite imagination and encourage expression. Many pages are ready for duplication.

Lipson, Greta B. and Baxter Morrison. FACT, FANTASY AND FOLKLORE. Good Apple, 1977.

A collection of challenging creative thinking and expressing ideas built around twelve well-known fairy tales. Highly recommended for gifted kids and others above third grade.

Maid, Amy and Roger Wallace. NOT JUST SCHOOLWORK. Mandala, 1976.

Ready-to-duplicate (or to use otherwise) experiences planned to strengthen writing skills and creative thinking. It's a whole writing curriculum! For grades 4 and up, with specific applicability to junior high school students.

MAKING IT STRANGE. Harper and Row, 1968.

A series of four workbooks for kids. Each is a series of lessons in original and metaphorical thinking and writing. (The series has a teacher's guide as well.)

Hassett, Jo and Charlene Whisnant. POETRY POWER: IDEAS FOR CREATIVE WRITING. Red Clay Books, 1973.

A small, inexpensive book just packed with fresh and interesting topics and starters for creative writing. It also shares some children's poetry and the wisdom of the teachers who helped them write it.

Manchester, Richard B. THE MAMMOTH BOOK OF WORD GAMES. Hart, 1978.

A fat compilation of fun and challenging write-in puzzles, codes and tricks with words. Written for adults . . . but most games are very usable for kids. Especially challenging for your gifted thinkers.

"Nose for News." INSTRUCTOR MAGAZINE, November, 1976.

An excellent 8-page handbook of ideas for writing newspapers with kids—done in the form of a newspaper.

Stanish, Bob. SUNFLOWERING. Good Apple, 1977.

In a class all by itself . . . an assortment of different, fresh instigators of original thinking and writing. If you want kids to look at usual things in unusual ways, and especially if you work with gifted kids, take a look at this one!

Wayman, Joe and Lorraine Plum. SECRETS AND SURPRISES. Good Apple, 1977.

Each idea begins with a movement activity, then suggests several follow-up exercises in the expression areas. These are great starters for writing and original thinking. Especially good for the elementary grades.

Wermuth, Linda. IMAGINATION AND LANGUAGE. Prentice-Hall, 1976.

Activities for upper elementary and junior high school writers. The emphasis is on writing skills and imaginative use of words. Pages are designed to be duplicated.

AND . . . FOR CONTENT AREA IDEAS THAT INSPIRE WRITING, LOOK AT:

Abruscato, Joe and Jack Hassard.   LOVING AND BEYOND: SCIENCE TEACHING FOR THE HUMANISTIC CLASSROOM.   Goodyear, 1976.

————.   THE WHOLE COSMOS CATALOG.   Goodyear, 1977.

Allison, Linda.   BLOOD AND GUTS: A WORKING GUIDE TO YOUR OWN INSIDES.   Little, Brown and Company, 1976.

————.   THE REASONS FOR SEASONS.   Little, Brown and Company, 1975.

————.   THE SIERRA CLUB SUMMER BOOK.   Charles Scribner's Sons, 1977.

Amazing Life Games Company.   GOOD CENTS: EVERY KID'S GUIDE TO MAKING MONEY.   Houghton Mifflin, 1974.

Burns, Marilyn.   I AM NOT A SHORT ADULT: GETTING GOOD AT BEING A KID.   Little, Brown and Company, 1977.

————.   THE I HATE MATHEMATICS BOOK.   Little, Brown and Company, 1975.

Donahue, Parnell and Helen Capellaro.   GERMS MAKE ME SICK!   Alfred A. Knopf, 1975.

Frank, Marjorie.   I CAN MAKE A RAINBOW: THINGS TO MAKE AND DO, FOR CHILDREN AND THEIR GROWN UP FRIENDS.   Incentive, 1976.

Forte, Imogene and Joy MacKenzie.   KIDS' STUFF SOCIAL STUDIES.   Incentive, 1976.

————.   OF RHINOCEROS WINGS AND MORE USUAL THINGS: CREATIVE ARTS FOR THE VERY YOUNG CHILD.   Incentive, 1978.

Weitzman, David.   MY BACKYARD HISTORY BOOK.   Little, Brown and Company, 1975.

Wurman, Richard Saul.   THE YELLOW PAGES OF LEARNING RESOURCES.   Group for Environmental Education, 1972.

SPECIAL BOOKS FOR STIMULATING WRITING AND SPREADING LOVE FOR LANGUAGE

Tricks and Fun With WORDS . . . . . .

Doty, Roy. GUNGA, YOUR DIN-DIN IS READY. Doubleday, 1976.

A book full of charmingly illustrated puns, riddles, gags and quips.

Emrich, Duncan. RIDDLES, JOKES AND FOOLISH FACTS. Scholastic, 1973.

A paperback collection of word plays, riddles and silly advice.

Hayward, Linda. LETTERS, SOUNDS AND WORDS. Platt and Munk, 1973.

A phonics book and creative dictionary that contains, for each letter and a number of letter combinations, a most imaginative string of alliterative sounds.

Hunt, Bernice. YOUR ANT IS A WHICH. Harcourt, Brace, Jovanovich, 1968.

A beginner's book of homophones—written in poetry.

Kuskin, Karla. ROAR AND MORE. Harper Row, 1956.

Verses about the sounds of animals—written for kids to join in when it's time to make the sound.

Miller, Albert G. BACKWARD BEASTS. Bowmar, 1974.

Each page turns an animal's name backwards and creates a new animal. New animal collage illustrations are accompanied by poems.

Morrison, Bill. SQUEEZE A SNEEZE. Houghton Mifflin, 1971.

Fun, sensible nonsense that inspires kids to make up rhymes. Enjoyable for all ages.

Reid, Alastair. OUNCE, DICE, TRICE. Little, Brown and Company, 1958.

An unusual collection of word collections: words for grumbling or singing, names for elephants, words for counting, and more . . . A good stimulator for word collecting—for all ages.

Rosenbloom, Joseph. THE BIGGEST RIDDLE BOOK IN THE WORLD. Sterling, 1976.

Exactly what it says—2000 of the best and worst riddles ever invented—about everything from astronauts to zebras. Great fun!

Tremain, Ruthuen. FOOLING AROUND WITH WORDS. Greenwillow Books, 1976.

An easy-to-read group of tricky ways that words can fool your eyes and ears. Written for beginning readers.

* *

✷ *Very Good For Inspiring Imaginative Thinking . . . . . .*

Barrett, Judith. ANIMALS SHOULD DEFINITELY NOT WEAR CLOTHING. Atheneum, 1970.

Everybody will enjoy this projection of what might happen if animals wore clothes.

Baylor, Byrd. EVERYBODY NEEDS A ROCK. Charles Scribner's Sons, 1974.

A rock-lover tells ten rules for finding and loving your very own special rock. A good writing stimulator.

————. SOMETIMES I DANCE MOUNTAINS. Charles Scribner's Sons, 1973.

Unusual artwork and a few words show a child creating worlds and feelings with her body. A good beginning for creative movement that can lead to writing.

Carle, Eric. I SEE A SONG. Thomas Y. Crowell, 1973.

A story of a musician's performance—told in colors instead of words. Kids can create the phrases to match.

DeMille, Richard. PUT YOUR MOTHER ON THE CEILING. Viking, 1973.

A series of exercises designed to stretch imaginations. It gets kids thinking of circumstances that don't ordinarily exist, and can be a motivator of writing fantasies.

Forte, Imogene and Joy MacKenzie. TRY SQUIGGLES AND SQUIRMS AND WIGGLY WORMS. Incentive, 1978.

A book about all the kinds of things you can do with your body. It gets kids moving and feeling and pretending and imagining. For very young children (preschool) but very usable through grades 1 and 2.

Grimm, Gary, et al. DANDYLIONS NEVER ROAR. Good Apple, 1973.

————. IMAGINATION AND ME. Good Apple, 1976.

Two records, with accompanying activity books, that are filled with songs and questions to prod imaginative thinking, doing and writing.

Gwynne, Fred. A CHOCOLATE MOOSE FOR DINNER. Windmill, 1976.

————. THE KING WHO RAINED. Windmill, 1972.

Both belong in every classroom! They are collections of fantastically illustrated idioms: expressions that, if taken literally, would be absolutely ridiculous!

Hoban, Tana. LOOK AGAIN! Macmillan, 1971.

A no-word book of surprises that gives visual experiences in looking at ordinary things in an extraordinary way.

Anglund, Joan Walsh. CHRISTMAS IS A TIME OF GIVING. Harcourt Brace, 1961.

————. A FRIEND IS SOMEONE WHO LIKES YOU. Harcourt Brace, 1958.

————. LOVE IS A SPECIAL WAY OF FEELING. Harcourt Brace, 1960.

————. SPRING IS A NEW BEGINNING. Harcourt Brace, 1963.

Each of her warm, poetic little books shares honest and universal feelings that serve as starters for kids to think and talk about the big meanings of life.

Buscaglia, Leo. BECAUSE I AM HUMAN. Charles B. Slack, 1972.

A book-length poem about what a fine thing it is to be human.

Carle, Eric. THE VERY HUNGRY CATERPILLAR. Collins, 1969.

A beautifully written and illustrated life story of a caterpillar. Especially appealing for young listeners, who may wish to invent details of their own to add to the story.

Charlip, Remy. FORTUNATELY. Parents' Magazine Press, 1966.

A delightful tale that switches from good fortune to bad again and again.

————. MOTHER, MOTHER I FEEL SICK, SEND FOR THE DOCTOR QUICK QUICK QUICK. Parents' Magazine Press, 1964.

The ridiculous tale—in poetry—of a lad who ate the most surprising things!

Emerich, Duncan. THE HODGEPODGE BOOK. Four Winds Press, 1972.

Everything from how to cure freckles to knock-knock jokes to how to make an elephant float. It's a collection of out-of-the-ordinary information from American folklore. It will inspire kids to write their own jokes, riddles, puzzles, advice and conundrums.

Horwitz, Elinor Lander. WHEN THE SKY IS LIKE LACE. J. B. Lippincott, 1975.

This delicate book is about an unusual, mysterious happening. The language makes listeners hear velvet, feel music and taste lavender.

Keats, Ezra Jack. DREAMS. Macmillan, 1974.

After everyone—or almost everyone—is asleep, a paper mouse takes on special powers. A good book for starting young writers thinking about dreams.

THE KIDS' STUFF ACTIVITY RECORD. Incentive, 1973.

It's a get-involved record that draws children into creating stories and naming sounds and dramatizing situations. Excellent for preschool–grade 3.

Lionni, Leo. FREDERICK. Pantheon, 1968.

One mouse dreams and imagines while the others work. Then, in the cold days of winter, he shares the poetry of his daydreams.

————. SWIMMY. Pantheon, 1963.

An imaginative little fish uses his creativity to solve a big problem. This is a story to stimulate writing about original solutions.

Martel, Jane. SMASHED POTATOES. Houghton Mifflin, 1974.

A compilation of original recipes dictated to an adult by children too young to write. You'll delight in hearing how to make everything from skabbetti to banilla cake.

Mayer, Mercer. ONE MONSTER AFTER ANOTHER. Golden Press, 1976.

To start original tales and verses about monsters, read your writers this story about lovable and very unusual monsters.

————. THERE'S A NIGHTMARE IN MY CLOSET. Dial Press, 1968.

This account of a boy's relationship with the nightmare in his closet can start kids talking about their nighttime fears.

O'Neill, Mary. HAILSTONES AND HALIBUT BONES. Doubleday, 1961.

A must for every classroom! It's a wonderful stimulator for translating color into sights and sounds and smells and tastes and feelings.

Pinkwater, Daniel Manus. THE BIG ORANGE SPLOT. Hastings House, 1977.

Mr. Plumbean pops his cork . . . and changes his world in this story. It will inspire kids to write and talk about how small risks create big changes.

Schwartz, Alvin. CROSS YOUR FINGERS, SPIT IN YOUR HAT: SUPERSTITIONS AND BELIEFS. Lippincott, 1974.

————. TOMFOOLERY: TRICKERY AND FOOLERY WITH WORDS. Lippincott, 1973.

————. A TWISTER OF TWISTS, A TANGLER OF TONGUES. Lippincott, 1972.

————. WHOPPERS: TALL TALES AND OTHER LIES. Lippincott, 1975.

————. WITCRACKS: JOKES AND JESTS FROM AMERICAN FOLKLORE. Lippincott, 1973.

Five of my favorites! They're filled with lies, superstitions, cures, omens, advice, ribticklers, riddles, outlandish tales, rhymes, games and twisters from American folklore. They can start dozens of writing activities in classrooms—for all ages.

Seuling, Barbara. YOU CAN'T EAT PEANUTS IN CHURCH AND OTHER LITTLE-KNOWN LAWS. Dolphin, 1975.

The author has collected strange and amusing laws that were written at some point in history (and are still on the books!). Kids will enjoy writing their own or making up explanations for these.

Viorst, Judith. ALEXANDER AND THE TERRIBLE, HORRIBLE, NO-GOOD, VERY BAD DAY. Atheneum, 1972.

A story for anyone of any age who has ever had an awful day.

————. ALEXANDER, WHO USED TO BE RICH LAST SUNDAY. Atheneum, 1978.

Every child will relate to Alexander's struggles with keeping money!

————. MY MAMA SAYS THERE AREN'T ANY ZOMBIES, GHOSTS, VAMPIRES, CREATURES, DEMONS, MONSTERS, FIENDS, GOBLINS OR THINGS. Atheneum, 1978.

A story to open up expression of fears about "things" in the dark and of doubts about adult assurances.

————. ROSIE AND MICHAEL. Atheneum, 1977.

A beautiful statement on what friendship really means.

————. THE TENTH GOOD THING ABOUT BARNEY. Atheneum, 1977.

Barney, the cat, has just died, and his family is eulogizing him by making a list of his good qualities.

Waber, Bernard. IRA SLEEPS OVER. Houghton Mifflin, 1972.

Max, who is going to spend the night with a friend, worries about whether or not he should take his teddy bear. A great tale about friends and security needs!

Zemach, Margot. THINGS COULD ALWAYS BE WORSE. Farrar, Straus, Giroux, 1976.

There is universal truth and a strong moral to this Yiddish tale about a man who is irritated by crowded conditions in his home.

Zolotow, Charlotte. DO YOU KNOW WHAT I'LL DO? Harper Row, 1958.

————. THE HATING BOOK. Harper Row, 1969.

————. IF IT WEREN'T FOR YOU. Harper Row, 1966.

————. IT'S NOT FAIR. Harper Row, 1976.

————. MY FRIEND JOHN. Harper Row, 1968.

These five and many others of Ms. Zolotow's books verbalize real and universal feelings that children have about friends, siblings, families, disappointments. They are all excellent beginnings for discussions and writings—for students of all ages.

FAVORITE COLLECTIONS OF POETRY

Abercrombie, Barbara, ed. THE OTHER SIDE OF A POEM. Harper Row, 1977.

Choice poems with high appeal, put together in enticing groupings with personal notes to the kids.

Adams, Adrienne. POETRY OF EARTH. Charles Scribner, 1972.

Poems about the earth and her creatures—for young readers.

Aiken, Conrad. CATS AND BATS AND THINGS WITH WINGS. Atheneum, 1965.

Creative observations about all kinds of animals—written in unusual shapes and forms. Beautifully illustrated.

Arbuthnot, May Hill and Shelton L. Root, eds. TIME FOR POETRY. Scott Foresman, 1968.

The most complete collection of all kinds of poetry on nearly every topic that I've found PLUS an excellent section on using poetry in the classroom.

Adoff, Arnold, ed. BLACK OUT LOUD. Dell, 1975.

Poems by black poets . . . meaningful and appealing to all children.

Brewton, Sara and John, eds. MY TANG'S TUNGLED AND OTHER RIDICULOUS SITUA-TIONS. Thomas Y. Crowell, 1973.

A delightful gathering of tongue twisters and silly poems.

Ciardi, John. THE REASON FOR THE PELICAN. J. B. Lippincott, 1959.

23 warm, ridiculous poems that kids will love.

————. YOU READ TO ME, I'LL READ TO YOU. J. B. Lippincott, 1962.

Humorous poems written to be read to kids. Every other poem is simple enough that a first grader can read it to you.

Cole, William. BEASTLY BOYS AND GHASTLY GIRLS. World, 1964.

Poems about things kids should never do—and about boys and girls who lead lives that are neither good nor dull.

————. OH, WHAT NONSENSE! Viking, 1966.

Hilarious rhymes and ridiculous pictures about things that never could happen.

Cullum, Albert. THE GERANIUM ON THE WINDOWSILL JUST DIED, BUT TEACHER YOU WENT RIGHT ON. Harlin Quist, 1971.

Poems for teachers which kids will enjoy too (if you have the nerve to expose the foibles of teachers!).

Dunning, Stephen, *et al.*, **eds.** REFLECTIONS ON A GIFT OF WATERMELON PICKLE. Lothrop, 1969.

One of my favorite collections of poems that are chosen carefully for young people. A varied selection, relevant to kids' interests.

————. SOME HAYSTACKS DON'T EVEN HAVE ANY NEEDLES. Lothrop, 1969.

Poems about the real world . . . chosen for older students.

Frank, Josette. POEMS TO READ TO THE VERY YOUNG. Random, 1969.

Simple, nicely-illustrated poems for little children.

Frost, Robert. YOU COME TOO. Holt, Rinehart and Winston, 1959.

A group of Frost's poems especially chosen to be read to and by young people.

Fujikawa, Gyo. A CHILD'S BOOK OF POEMS. Grosset and Dunlap, 1969.

A lovely book of well-chosen poems with special appeal to young children. Preschool-grade 3.

Giovanni, Nikki. EGO TRIPPING AND OTHER POEMS FOR YOUNG READERS. Lawrence Hill, 1973.

Poems about being black and about being human— recommended for grades 5 and up.

Hopkins, Lee Bennet, ed. THE CITY SPREADS ITS WINGS. Franklin Watts, 1970.

20 poems about the people, sounds, sights, feelings and moods of the city—selected for young children.

Hughes, Langston. DON'T YOU TURN BACK. Alfred A. Knopf, 1969.

Selected Hughes poems about love, hate, dreams, hope, despair—in today's language. Strong appeal for jr. high and older.

ILLUSTRATED POEMS FOR CHILDREN. Rand Press, 1973.

The best and most beautiful anthology I've discovered for young children. It is arranged and illustrated superbly and exposes the reader to many styles—including Blake and Mother Goose.

Larrick, Nancy, ed. ON CITY STREETS.   M. Evans, 1968.

A fine collection of enjoyable poems about the experiences and inhabitants and scenes of the city—well-chosen for youngsters.

Lear, Edward. COMPLETE NONSENSE OF EDWARD LEAR.   Dover, 1951.

A huge collection of crazy, zany poems—mostly limericks!

Leuders, Edward, *et al.*, **eds.** ZERO MAKES ME HUNGRY.   Lothrop, 1976.

By the editors of Watermelon Pickle, another book full of poems that are alive and powerful and relevant to young readers. Especially recommended for intermediate and older.

Lewis, Richard. MIRACLES: POEMS BY CHILDREN OF THE ENGLISH-SPEAKING WORLD.   Simon and Schuster, 1966.

Poems written by children from many countries—ages 5-13. They reveal the rich imaginations and command of the language that children have and act as inspiration for your students.

McCord, David. EVERY TIME I CLIMB A TREE.   Little, Brown and Company, 1967.

Poems that the youngest readers will want to hear and say again and again.

Merriam, Eve. IT DOESN'T ALWAYS HAVE TO RHYME.   Atheneum, 1964.

Ms. Merriam does unique, delightful things with words. Her plays with sound and rhythm and metaphor will inspire your students to love and write poetry.

Ness, Evaline. AMELIA MIXED THE MUSTARD AND OTHER POEMS.   Scribners, 1975.

20 outrageous poems about silly girls. Beautifully illustrated.

Silverstein, Shel. WHERE THE SIDEWALK ENDS.   Harper Row, 1974.

Kids of all ages (and grown-ups too) love these fun poems about curiosity, naughtiness, mix-ups, warnings and much more. Every classroom needs a copy of this book!

Stopple, Libby. A BOX OF PEPPERMINTS.   American Universal Artforms, 1975.

Written from a child's point of view, this collection of poems touches on the everyday things in a child's life: grandma, animals, getting in trouble, parents, old people, God. Really enjoyable for the earlier grades.

Sendak, Maurice. CHICKEN SOUP WITH RICE.   Scholastic, 1970.

A short, rhymed story about the seasons for very young children. The best part about it is that the kids can easily join in on the refrain.

Zaslow, David. SOMEDAYS IT FEELS LIKE IT WANTS TO RAIN.   Onset Publications, 1976.

An inexpensive little paperback containing poems about such things as feelings and ice cream and blue jeans. It is the source of some especially lovely metaphors.

"How can I get them to write on their own?"

INDEPENDENCE

✳ In Celebration Of Independent Writing

✳ How To Help Them Do It On Their Own

✳ Personal Journals For Kids And Teachers

✳ A Plan For A Permanent Writing Center In Your Classroom

✳ 20 Mini-Centers You Can Make In Minutes

IN CELEBRATION OF INDEPENDENT WRITING

Karen and Suzie have been writing (and typing up) adventure stories all summer.

Tom has planted a limerick on his dad's desk every day for the last two weeks.

Kelly and friends write and sell a little publication called *What's Happening On Westgate Avenue?* to neighbors. (They sell advertising space, too.)

Teachers at Hawthorne School find little rhymes hanging over their doorknobs on Valentine's Day—left by a stealthy band of first graders.

Eighth graders at Hamburg Junior High School write *Dear Blabby,* letters and get advice from a team of anonymous "counselors" (their peers).

Jacob has started carrying on a correspondence in code with the principal.

Mary Anne stashes in the back of her desk a whole portfolio of private poetry.

Paul comes to school one morning and hands Ms. Ashley, his first grade teacher, an unsolicited poem written on a napkin. His mother testifies to his sole and spontaneous authorship of the piece.

Andrea and Tom write weekly sports reviews and predictions for outcomes of weekend games—and distribute them to fellow sports fans.

Kids do it all the time! Without adult suggestion or supervision, they're writing profusely—original plays and puppet shows, letters to Santa Claus, sidewalk graffiti, invitations to secret club meetings, signs to hang on their desks or in their lockers, love notes, hate notes and secrets to pass across the room.

Because I'm convinced that growth is stimulated and challenge offered by teacher-initiated writing experiences, and because I rejoice for the good times kids have writing in the presence of a skilled guide, this book outlines plans for structuring and ideas for launching group sessions. But such beliefs neither exclude the spontaneous nor assume that good writing emerges only from formal lessons. I applaud the self-initiated expressions of children and praise the teachers who encourage them.

Observing and eavesdropping on teachers skilled at keeping alive and building upon the natural motivations to write has taught me that it's done by

    . . . providing time and avenues within the school day for independent writing

    . . . encouraging kids to start scrapbooks, collections, folders, private journals, diaries, portfolios

    . . . creating settings in which students can share or tell about that personal writing

    . . . using those pieces as motivators or beginnings for class writing experiences

    . . . the teacher's participating in his own independent writing (in ways that kids can notice it)

        by: writing notes to kids and other teachers

           making signs and banners for his own desk

           letting students see personal reminders he writes to himself

           posting a protest sign on occasion

           writing messages in the dirt to kids at recess

I understand
That the animals are not friendly
And the men of the world
Can be seen from miles away.

I see
The moon's lonely light
Will be there
Forever.

          Paul Dasaro
          Age—almost 6

HOW TO HELP THEM DO IT ON THEIR OWN

Capitalizing on their unsolicited works gives a head start to the teaching of independence in writing. Then what about continuing the process within the classroom?

> ### BIAS #19   INDEPENDENCE IS CULTIVATED
> *Freedom and time to write alone are the fertile soil. But teachers can offer a great deal more to nourish the growth of competent, autonomous writers: patterns and tools for independent writing plus experience in using the tools <u>before</u> they're sent off on their own.*

FIRST ... Be sure they write with a teacher-assisted group often enough to gain security in the writing process.

... Present them with a pattern to follow for writing and reinforce the procedure regularly.

... Make available aids for independent editing, proofreading and evaluating. Keep these close at hand for easy use.

... Gather kids together from time to time for drilling on the skills they need for writing and rewriting on their own.

THEN ... They'll know what steps to follow: how to find ideas, stretch them and change them into words.

... They'll know where to look for assistance when they need it.

... They'll have their supplies packed for trekking off on independent adventures and investigating challenges in writing centers.

The remaining sections of this chapter suggest means for instigating and organizing independent writing activities within the classroom. The PERSONAL JOURNAL PLAN gets kids (and you) writing on their own DAILY—about anything! The design for a CLASSROOM WRITING CENTER is intended to spur you to create a place that centralizes tools, aids and ideas as well as provides a place for private writing in the room. And the MINI-CENTERS are examples of everyday items that, with a little ingenuity and not too much time, can be turned into suppliers of writing starters for use without teacher aid.

Although I am an ardent crusader for individualized instruction and an avid user of learning centers, I believe that "independent" or "individualized" aids to writing can be easily misused—or at least used in ways that diminish their value. I don't think you _teach_ a student to write on her own by sending her to a writing corner (no matter how attractive it may be). Nor do you advance a student's writing skills by giving him a soup can full of inventive soup-related ideas and saying, "Choose one." The soup can or corner are not, by themselves, the motivators. Kids need an introduction to them and a reason for using them!

So when you set up a permanent writing center in the classroom, do it with the help of the students. Let them create the aids and reminders for writing skills and processes. Make sure they are thoroughly acquainted with the contents of the center and the procedures for using it. Put into your Writer's Nook tasks that have grown out of other activities students have done together.

After a great lie-telling party or whopper-writing session, the time will be ripe for starting a YOU'LL NEVER BELIEVE _____ collection in the writing center. You might ask that each student add one page sometime during the next week.

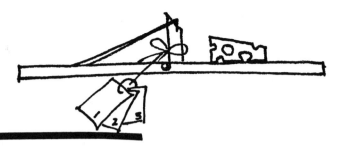

And when students are ready for independent starters such as those suggested in the MINI-CENTER section of this chapter,

INTEGRATE THE CENTER INTO OTHER CLASSROOM EXPERIENCES.

A mouse trap or trash can full of writing ideas may seem irrelevant or uninviting to students. But if the mouse trap, with its writing starters, appears the day you've shared your favorite "mice" poem or the day after a mouse has been loose in the room—or if the group begins filling a trash can with junk and using the "Straight From The Trash Can" ideas during a science unit in ecology, the purpose of the mini-center will be much clearer.

INTRODUCE THE CENTER.

Everyone (even those who don't use it) should know the contents and expectations for each individualized activity available in the classroom. The introductions can be made by the student who created the center or by the teacher.

INCLUDE OPTIONS WITHIN EACH CENTER.

Offer enough kinds and levels of tasks within each to suit the abilities and enliven the interests of many writers.

INVOLVE THE STUDENTS IN CREATING THE OPTIONS.

Ask the kids to add at least one idea each time they use a center. Or, suggest the basic idea for a mini-center, and have students create ALL the options.

PERSONAL JOURNALS FOR KIDS AND TEACHERS

> ### BIAS #20   PERSONAL WRITING MEETS
> ### HUMAN NEEDS
> One of the best reasons for writing on your own is
> that writing (even if, and especially when, it's not in-
> tended for an audience) serves as an excellent outlet
> for feelings and ideas.

It's a good way to try out your convictions, or get a clear look
at dilemmas, or vent hostilities, or examine your fears, or articulate
feelings. It's a good way to get to know yourself. And private writing
lets you do all this without the risk of trying out thoughts on someone else!

Several years ago I met a first grade teacher at a workshop who
turned me on to the joys and successes and fulfillment of using personal journals in the classroom. Since then, I've heard and experienced so much good news about the method's contribution to personal expression and writing enthusiasm that I'm encouraging you to
try it too! Here are some ideas for getting started:

* Get a notebook for each student—and yourself.

* Dedicate two, five or ten minutes DAILY to private writing.
  Choose different times, situations and settings each day so as
  to catch a variety of moods and ideas.

* Declare the journals off limits to everyone but the author.

* Let kids write in any form, on any topic. If they ask, you
  might suggest ideas: *Morning Feelings . . . Things Worth Saving . . . Skywatching . . . Dreams . . . If Only . . . I Could
  Never Do Without . . . I Worry About . . . Compliments . . . I
  Wonder Why . . .*

* Encourage them to carry their notebooks around for collecting words, ideas, snatched sentences, overheard dialogues, etc.

* Share one of your entries now and then. Encourage, but
  don't push students to share too. Often, they'll find that
  something they intended only for themselves turned out to
  be so good in writing that they'll want to read it aloud!

*...NGS KIDS HAVE SAID
...ME IN THE MORNING . .
...like my new dress?"
"What'd ya do to your
   hair?"
"Where were you yesterday?
"We had a big fight
at our house today!"
"Can I bring my
   dog to school ?"
"How many more
days 'til vacation?*

A PLAN FOR A PERMANENT WRITING CENTER IN YOUR CLASSROOM

Create a WRITER'S NOOK . . . SCRIBE'S CORNER . . . EDITOR'S DESK . . . WRITER'S HIDEAWAY . . .
(or whatever name your students choose)

. . . . . . *set up behind a screen or bookcase . . . in a large box . . . under a canopy . . . in a cozy corner . . . . . any place with a comfortable place to sit and think.*

. . . . . . *furnished with a writer's desk, preferably with drawers, . . . shelves for storing writing supplies . . . a bulletin or peg board for ideas . . . a large BILLBOARD or GALLERY WALL for sharing.*

. . . . . . *containing an assortment of activities . . . motivational devices . . . tools . . . aids . . . and ideas ready for use by young writers.*

. . . . . . *well-organized—with supplies stored in easily accessible places such as tiered boxes . . . tin cans . . . oatmeal boxes . . . round ice cream containers . . . etc.*

. . . . . . *changing and growing . . . a place where the supply of fresh ideas, progressively more sophisticated techniques and timely motivators is flowing freely.*

Your center might include:

✳ THINGS TO WRITE ON ...

plain paper	old notebooks	floors
newspaper	notepads	clear filmstrips
lined paper	envelopes	old boxes
newsprint	cardboard tubes	plaster of paris tablets
construction paper	slates	old plastic tablecloths
cardboard	old window shades	chalkboards
butcher paper	rocks	sand
graph paper	vinyl scraps	walls (covered with vinyl or paper)
carbon paper	fabric	bricks
paper bags	adding machine tape	shingles
file cards	wrapping paper	driftwood
plastic bags	window panes	bark

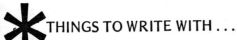 THINGS TO WRITE WITH ...

pencils	pens
crayons	markers
nails	feathers
fingers	yarn or string
cut-out letters	toothpicks
invisible inks:	inks
milk or lemon juice	
chalk	
brushes and paints	
typewriter	
rubber stamps and stamp pad	
word and phrases cut from	
newspapers or magazines	

> *Keep in this center the word collections and idea compilations that the class has gathered in earlier lessons or word-play games. When students use these as aids,*
>
> *— motivation increases because they're writing with ideas and tools they have invented or created.*
>
> *— independence is encouraged because they're using the aid on their own.*
>
> *— YOU are freed from the burden of being the sole source of ideas and inspiration.*
>
> *— they are building new writing experiences on previous ones—and that's what growth is all about!*

OTHER WRITER'S TOOLS . . .

stapler	rulers	contac paper
notebook rings	clipboard	erasers
scissors	foil	tape recorder
dictionary	thesaurus	synonym dictionary
spelling lists	glue	paper fasteners

WRITER'S AIDS . . .

Word Lists:

food words	*color words*	*feeling words*	
number words	*city words*	*sound words*	
people words	*helping words*	*outdoor words*	*etc. . .*

A list of the steps to follow when you write

Checklist for editing

Checklist for proofreading

Questions to ask yourself about your finished product

Proper forms or "formulas" for different kinds of writing:

limericks	*haiku*	*business letters*	
cinquains	*sestinas*	*friendly letters*	
diamantes	*couplets*	*sonnets*	*etc. . .*

Examples of:

advertisements	*editorials*	*concrete poems*	
invitations	*announcements*	*letters*	
headlines	*telegrams*	*dialogues*	
news articles	*interviews*	*sports reports*	*etc. . .*
travel brochures	*thank you notes*		

Chart on how to make a book

Suggestions for sharing writing

* AND LOTS OF WRITING STARTERS . . . . . . HERE ARE JUST A FEW . . . . . .

Original Books (student composites) to which they can add a page or poem or line . . .

Lion Tales	*Close Encounters*
Yummy Book	*WHY? Book*
Horrorscopes	*Creature Features*
HELP!	*Letters to God*
Our Pet Peeves	*Imagine That!*
Rebus Stories	*Good News-Bad News Stories*
Just Plain Good Advice	*Our Dilly Dictionary of Daffy Definitions*
Our Own Book of World Records	*Who's Who in our School*
You'll Never Believe	*Our Undeniably Wise Sayings*
A Principal Is	*Yours Till . . . . . .*
Our Book of Lists	*Trips You Should Take*
Slips of the Tongue	*Cures for Common (and Uncommon) Diseases*

Take-A-Title Can

Story Dials (i.e.: Dial a character, setting, situation)

Cliff Hangers to Finish

Hot Line of Bright Ideas (each idea written on a light bulb)

Grab Bag of Story Ideas

Addresses for Letter Writing

Spider Web of Words (Choose 5 words to "weave" into a blood-curdling tale.)

News Headlines (YOU write the article.)

News Articles (YOUwrite the headline.)

FBI CARD FILE of Clues for Who-Done-It Stories

Nonsense Words to Define

What If . . . . . . Card File

Cartoons and Comic Strips without Captions

STRAIGHT FROM THE TRASH CAN

WRITE A PROPOSAL TO YOUR FAMILY TELLING WAYS THEY CAN CUT DOWN ON WASTE.

BUILD A GARBAGE GLOSSARY. WRITE DEFINITIONS OF WORDS THAT HAVE TO DO WITH TRASH. DESIGN A COVER FOR YOUR DICTIONARY.

CHOOSE ONE JUNK. WRITE TEN WORDS THAT TELL ABOUT ITS SIZE, SHAPE, SMELL, FEEL, COLOR, USE.

FOR EACH LETTER OF THE WORD GARBAGE, WRITE A WORD THAT COULD DESCRIBE TRASH.

WRITE A CAREFUL DESCRIPTION OF ONE OF THE ITEMS IN THIS CAN, BUT DO NOT MENTION ITS NAME. SEE IF SOMEONE ELSE CAN TELL WHICH JUNK IT IS.

WHICH PIECE OF TRASH IS WORTH THE MOST? WRITE TEN REASONS WHY IT IS THE MOST VALUABLE.

CHOOSE ONE JUNK. TELL SIX WAYS IT COULD BE USED.

FOR EACH PIECE OF JUNK, WRITE ONE SENTENCE EXPLAINING WHY IT WAS THROWN AWAY.

WRITE A CONVERSATION BETWEEN TWO OF THE PIECES OF TRASH.

WRITE A LIE ABOUT ONE PIECE OF JUNK.

CHOOSE TWO PIECES OF TRASH. TELL HOW THEY ARE ALIKE.

WRITE A BUMPER STICKER THAT WILL ENCOURAGE PEOPLE NOT TO THROW AWAY ONE OF THE PIECES OF JUNK.

WRITE A LOVE STORY ABOUT TWO OF THE ITEMS.

WRITE A POEM ABOUT A BOY WHO WOULDN'T TAKE OUT THE GARBAGE.

CHOOSE ONE JUNK. WRITE TEN QUESTIONS IT WOULD ASK IF IT COULD TALK.

WRITE A DESCRIPTION OF THE FAMILY WHO OWNS THIS TRASH CAN. WHAT DOES THEIR TRASH TELL ABOUT THEM?

WRITE SOME RIDDLES ABOUT JUNK!

WRITE A MENU FOR A MEAL THAT CAN BE PREPARED USING THINGS PEOPLE USUALLY THROW AWAY.

WRITE A JOB DESCRIPTION FOR A GARBAGE COLLECTOR.

WHAT JUNK FROM THIS CAN WOULD YOU LIKE TO KEEP? WRITE YOUR REASONS.

MAKE A LIST OF 15 EXCUSES FOR NOT TAKING OUT THE TRASH.

WRITE A HILARIOUS JUNK JOKE.

WRITE A POEM THAT HAS THE NAME OF A PIECE OF JUNK IN EVERY LINE.

WRITE A LIST OF RULES FOR A CONTEST TO SEE WHICH CLASS IN YOUR SCHOOL CAN THROW AWAY THE LEAST AMOUNT OF STUFF IN A WEEK.

THINK OF THE YUKKIEST PIECE OF TRASH YOU'VE EVER SEEN. OR FIND AND LOOK AT A REALLY ICKY ONE! NOW . . . WRITE A SENTENCE OR POEM OR DESCRIPTION THAT MAKES THAT GARBAGE SEEM BEAUTIFUL!

WRITE THE GREATEST GARBAGE STORY EVER TOLD.

WRITE A QUESTIONNAIRE THAT YOU AND YOUR CLASSMATES CAN USE FOR TAKING A SURVEY OF WHAT'S BEING WASTED IN YOUR SCHOOL.

CHOOSE ONE JUNK. TELL WHAT THE WORLD IS LIKE NOW THAT IT'S GONE.

20 MINI-CENTERS YOU CAN MAKE IN MINUTES

One interesting object
+ Several writing tasks
(on separate cards)
_____
= Loads of appealing
motivators —
all in one container.

Make cards in the shape of mice!

IS COKE THE REAL THING?

"SHOULD COKE BE SOLD?" WRITE AN ANSWER TO THIS QUESTION FROM THE VIEWPOINT OF A NUTRITIONIST, A 3RD GRADER, A 3RD GRADER'S MOTHER, A DENTIST OR A COCA COLA COMPANY PRESIDENT.

WRITE THE SCRIPT OF A DEBATE BETWEEN AN ANTI-SODA NUTRITIONIST AND A COKE FAN.

WRITE A GOOD NEWS-BAD NEWS STORY ABOUT COKE.

WRITE A LETTER TO THE COCA COLA COMPANY PROTESTING THE MANUFACTURE OF COKE.

WRITE SOME PROVERBS ABOUT COKE.

Write A GUIDE TO SODA POP DRINKING for kids.

HOW DOES COKE SOUND? WRITE TEN SOUND WORDS.

DOES "COKE ADD LIFE?" WRITE FIVE REASONS WHY IT DOES OR DOESN'T.

FINISH THESE:
Drinking Coke is like _____
Coke tastes as _____ *as* _____

MAKE A CALORIE CHART FOR 15 OR MORE BEVERAGES.

WRITE A RECIPE FOR A NEW DRINK.

MOUSE TALES

FINISH THIS LIMERICK:
A mouse was exploring our house

_____

He awakened the cat
And _____

FINISH THIS RHYME:
Mice go after crumbs and cheese

INVENT TEN NAMES FOR A MOUSE.
WRITE DIRECTIONS FOR HOW TO CATCH A MOUSE.
MAKE A MOUSE ENCYCLOPEDIA OF INFORMATION ABOUT MICE.
WRITE A NEWS ARTICLE TELLING HOW A MOUSE SAVED THE CITY OF CHICAGO FROM DISASTER.
FOR EACH LETTER OF THE WORD MOUSE, WRITE A SENTENCE THAT TELLS SOMETHING ABOUT MICE.
WRITE A SPEECH TO A PERSON WHO'S AFRAID OF MICE. PRETEND YOU ARE THE MOUSE. TELL THE PERSON WHY HE/SHE SHOULDN'T BE AFRAID OF YOU.

201

❧❧ MENU ❧❧

YOUR ORDER, PLEASE?

FIND 20 WORDS ON THE MENU THAT APPEAL TO YOUR SENSE OF TASTE. ADD 10 MORE TO THE LIST.

WRITE A MENU AND DESCRIPTION FOR THE "SPECIAL OF THE DAY."

WRITE A MOUTH-WATERING DESCRIPTION OF ONE OF THE DESSERTS ON THE MENU.

ADD SOME TASTY SUGGESTIONS TO THE MENU. DESCRIBE EACH.
ie: Add a new beverage.
       Describe a new soup.
       Add a breakfast suggestion.

WRITE A CHILDREN'S MENU FOR THIS RESTAURANT.

WRITE A NEW GAME FOR THE BACK COVER OF THE MENU.

THIS IS A MENU FOR A TRUCK STOP. DESIGN A MENU FOR A RESTAURANT THAT CATERS TO BANKERS OR HULA DANCERS OR SURFERS OR PLUMBERS.

WRITE A JINGLE FOR THE RADIO THAT WOULD ADVERTISE THIS RESTAURANT.

DESIGN A NEW MENU FOR A:

Sandwich Shoppe	Sausage Hut	Seafood Shanty
Waffle House	Avacado Pit	Yogurt Bar
Crepe Shop	Pizza Palace	Onion House
Ice Cream Saloon	Hamburger Haven	Steak Stop

CEREAL BOX SCRIPTS

WRITE AN EXPLANATION OF HOW TO FIX AND EAT A BOWL OF CEREAL.

WRITE THREE SENTENCES ABOUT THE EXPERIENCE OF EATING CEREAL, USING ONLY THE WORDS ON THIS BOX.

FOR EACH LETTER IN THE WORD <u>WHEATIES</u> WRITE A SENTENCE TELLING ABOUT A PERSON WHO EATS WHEATIES.

Wanda Watermelon is watching her weight.

"BREAKFAST OF CHAMPIONS" IS THE SLOGAN WHEATIES HAS USED FOR YEARS. MAKE UP A NEW SLOGAN FOR WHEATIES.

WRITE A TONGUE TWISTER USING SOME OF THE W AND V WORDS ON THE BOX.

THERE IS A MONEY-BACK GUARANTEE ON THE BOX. WRITE A LETTER TO THE MANUFACTURER TELLING WHY YOU WANT YOUR MONEY BACK.

CREATE A CROSSWORD PUZZLE USING ONLY THE WORDS ON THIS BOX.

TELL HOW IT FEELS TO BE A BOWL OF CEREAL BEING EATEN BY A KID.

WRITE A LETTER ORDERING THE SPORTS BAG ON THE BACK OF THE BOX.

WRITE A RIDDLE OR A JOKE ABOUT THE INGREDIENTS IN WHEATIES.

FINISH THESE SIMILES:

Pouring cereal sounds like_____

Wheaties are as crisp as _____

_____ is like eating cereal

because _____

Eating Wheaties makes me feel like _____

Write ideas on spoons

FROM THE MIXING BOWL

WRITE A MENU FOR A MEAL THAT CAN BE EATEN WITHOUT SILVERWARE.
WRITE A RECIPE FOR A PEANUT-BUTTER BANANA MILKSHAKE.
WRITE A MENU FOR A PROGRESSIVE DINNER FOR DIABETICS.
WRITE A RECIPE BOOK OF HEALTHY SNACKS FOR KIDS.
WRITE A BREAKFAST MENU FOR 3-YEAR OLDS.
WRITE A PICNIC MENU FOR VEGETARIANS.
WRITE A MENU FOR A BIRTHDAY PARTY.
WRITE A RECIPE FOR A THUNDERSTORM.
WRITE A RECIPE FOR HAPPINESS PIE.
WRITE A RECIPE FOR DINOSAUR DIP.
WRITE A MENU FOR A YELLOW MEAL.
WRITE A RECIPE FOR A RAINBOW.
WRITE A RECIPE FOR TACOS.
WRITE A RECIPE FOR MUD.

WHAT'S FOR LUNCH?

Note to the teacher: the directions on the cards in this lunchbox refer to pictures of food that are included in the box and to pictures of people that have been glued on some of the cards.

WRITE 10 DESCRIBING WORDS FOR ONE OF THE FOODS. THINK ABOUT HOW IT TASTES, SOUNDS, SMELLS, LOOKS AND FEELS IN YOUR MOUTH.

THIS COWBOY IS ASKING FOR LUNCH. WRITE DOWN HIS ORDER.

WRITE A RECIPE FOR THIS DOG'S LUNCH.

FOR EACH FOOD ITEM, TELL IN WHOSE LUNCHBOX IT MIGHT BE FOUND. WRITE YOUR EXPLANATION OF WHY IN A SENTENCE.

WRITE A LUNCH MENU FOR THIS FAMILY.

CHOOSE FIVE FOODS. FOR EACH ONE, WRITE A SENTENCE THAT DESCRIBES THE FOOD IN A WAY THAT MAKES IT SOUND AWFUL.

WRITE A POEM THAT WILL CONVINCE KIDS TO EAT ONE OF THE FOODS.

TELL WHY THIS LADY PUT A BAG OVER HER HEAD AFTER LUNCH.

WRITE A WEEK OF LUNCH MENUS FOR THIS LADY.

WRITE A WEEK OF DIET MENUS FOR THIS MAN'S LUNCHES.

WRITE A LUNCH MENU FOR ONE OF THESE:

a barber	a steamshovel	an ant
a clown	a furnace	a bumblebee
your teacher	a python	a principal
a skyscraper		

SOUP'S ON

DESCRIBE A SOUP THAT WOULD BE EATEN BY AN ELEPHANT OR A SOUP FOR THE FUTURE OR A SOUP FOR A TRIP TO ANOTHER GALAXY

FOR EACH LETTER OF THE WORD SOUP, WRITE A SENTENCE TELLING ABOUT A KIND OF SOUP SOMEONE MIGHT EAT.

USE SIX WORDS FROM THIS SOUP CAN LABEL TO WRITE A TONGUE TWISTER.

Pickles, peas, parsley, potatoes and parmesan in a pan.

DESIGN A NEW LABEL FOR A CAN OF SOUP. MAKE UP YOUR OWN KIND OF SOUP. DON'T FORGET: THE SOUP NAME, INGREDIENTS, COMPANY NAME, DIRECTIONS FOR FIXING AND RECIPE IDEAS.

WRITE A RECIPE FOR A SOUP TO MAKE KIDS STRONG.

DESIGN A LABEL FOR PEANUT BUTTER SOUP OR MARSHMALLOW SOUP OR GRAVEL SOUP OR CREAMED GRAPE SOUP OR PUSSY WILLOW SOUP.

WRITE A POEM ABOUT THINGS THAT COME IN CANS.

JUMP-ROPE JINGLES

MAKE A LIST OF TEN GOOD WORDS FOR SAYING ALONG WITH JUMPING. (TRY *RUTABAGA!*)

WRITE A POEM TO SAY WHILE YOU JUMP ROPE.

MAKE A LIST OF J WORDS. THEN USE SOME OF THEM IN A JUMPING SONG.

WRITE A SHORT SPEECH THAT WILL EXPLAIN HOW TO JUMP ROPE (TO SOMEONE WHO DOESN'T KNOW HOW).

MAKE A LIST OF THINGS THAT JUMP. PUT THEM INTO A DICTIONARY OF JUMPIN' THINGS. FOR EACH ONE, DRAW A PICTURE AND WRITE A DESCRIPTION.

FINISH THESE SIMILES:

A twirling jumprope sounds like _____

When I jump, I feel as _____ *as a* _____

A jumprope is like July because _____

ACHOO!

FINISH THIS POEM:

*Of all the noses in the world
I'm glad that I have mine . . .*

_____
_____

WRITE THE LIFE STORY OF YOUR NOSE.

ON THIS BOX, WRITE WORDS THAT DESCRIBE KLEENEX.

MAKE A LIST OF WORDS THAT HAVE TO DO WITH COLDS AND SNEEZES.

CUT PICTURES OF NOSES OUT OF MAGAZINES. WRITE A SHORT PARAGRAPH FOR EACH NOSE TELLING HOW THAT NOSE HAS AFFECTED THE PERSON'S LIFE.

WRITE A POEM CALLED *Sneezes.*

MAKE A COLD CURE DIRECTORY. INCLUDE ALL THE INFORMATION YOU CAN FIND ABOUT PREVENTING OR RECOVERING FROM COLDS.

WRITE AN ANECDOTE TITLED: *Noses I Have Seen*

WRITE A TRIBUTE TO YOUR NOSE.

WRITE SOME EXAGGERATIONS THAT BEGIN: *One time I sneezed SO hard that* _____

MAKE A LIST OF 25 USES FOR A KLEENEX.

THINK OF TEN WORDS OR PHRASES THAT YOU COULD SAY WHEN A PERSON SNEEZES, OTHER THAN, "GOD BLESS YOU."

IF THE SHOE FITS

WRITE DOWN ALL THE FOOT SAYINGS YOU'VE HEARD. THEN MAKE UP SOME OF YOUR OWN.

WRITE A <u>SHOE</u> POEM. START THE FIRST LINE WITH S, THE SECOND WITH H, ETC.

WRITE AN ANECDOTE ABOUT A TIME YOU "PUT YOUR FOOT IN YOUR MOUTH."

DRAW AROUND YOUR FOOT AND CUT OUT YOUR FOOTPRINT. ON IT, WRITE ABOUT WHAT LIFE LOOKS LIKE FROM THE BOTTOM OF A FOOT.

WRITE A TRAVELOGUE AS THIS SHOE WOULD TELL IT.

WHAT CAN YOU TELL ABOUT THE OWNER OF THIS SHOE? WRITE A DESCRIPTION OF HER. TELL WHAT HER SHOE SHOWS ABOUT HER PERSONALITY.

WRITE ABOUT WHAT YOUR LIFE WOULD BE LIKE IF YOU SPENT A MONTH IN THE SHOES OF:

a mail person	your mother	a starving child	a toe dancer
a state senator	a coal miner	a crippled person	a mountain climber

WRITE A CONVERSATION BETWEEN A BOWLING SHOE AND A GLASS SLIPPER.

FINISH THESE:

New shoes make me feel _____

My old shoes smell as _____ as _____

Going without shoes is like _____

His shoes were tighter than _____

WRITE TEN SENTENCES USING THE WORD "SHOE." IN EACH ONE, USE THE WORD DIFFERENTLY. (A DICTIONARY CAN HELP.)

SCENES FROM A SLEEPING BAG

CLIMB IN THE BAG. HOW DOES IT FEEL? WRITE A LIST OF FEELING WORDS.

WHAT SOUNDS MIGHT YOU HEAR IN A SLEEPING BAG? WRITE A LIST OF SOUND WORDS.

WRITE ABOUT A DREAM YOU HAD IN A SLEEPING BAG.

WRITE THE LIFE STORY OF THIS ZIPPER.

WRITE ABOUT *The Camping Trip I'll Never Forget.*

DESCRIBE WHAT YOU SEE, FEEL, HEAR AND SMELL WHEN YOU WAKE UP IN THE MORNING LYING ON THE GROUND IN THE WOODS IN YOUR SLEEPING BAG.

WRITE AN ADVERTISEMENT FOR THIS BAG AS IT MIGHT APPEAR IN A KIDS' MAGAZINE.

WRITE A DIARY OF A THREE-DAY CAMP OUT.

WRITE A JOKE YOU MIGHT TELL A FRIEND WHEN YOU'RE IN YOUR SLEEPING BAGS IN A TENT.

WRITE A CONVERSATION BETWEEN TWO SLEEPING BAGS.
FINISH THESE SIMILES:

It is as warm as _____

It smells like _____

When I'm in the sleeping bag, I feel like _____

A sleeping bag is as _____ as a _____

Make cards in the shape of a foot!

205

TREASURES IN OLD MAGAZINES

CUT WORDS FROM THIS MAGAZINE TO WRITE A MYSTERY MESSAGE.

CUT OUT TWO PICTURES AND FOUR PHRASES FROM THIS MAGAZINE. USE ALL SIX OF THESE THINGS TO BUILD A STORY.

FIND A FOOD PICTURE. WRITE TEN WORDS THAT DESCRIBE THE FOOD. THEN DESCRIBE A PERSON WHO WOULD EAT IT.

WRITE FIVE PHRASES TO DESCRIBE THE FEELINGS THAT ARE SHOWN IN THE PICTURE ON PAGE 116.

WRITE THE CONVERSATION THAT IS GOING ON IN THE PICTURE ON PAGE 116.

WRITE A LIMERICK USING THREE WORDS YOU FIND IN THE AD ON PAGE 93.

WRITE A CAPTION FOR THE PICTURE ON PAGE 3.

LOOK AT THE PICTURE ON PAGE 99. TELL WHAT WILL HAPPEN NEXT.

PRETEND YOU ARE A FORTUNE TELLER. TELL THE FORTUNE OF THE LADY PICTURED ON PAGE 105.

WRITE A RIDDLE ABOUT THE PICTURE ON PAGE 124.

CUT WORDS OUT OF THIS MAGAZINE TO GIVE TO SOMEONE ELSE FOR CREATING A PROTEST.

I'VE GOT YOUR NUMBER

WRITE AN ADVERTISEMENT FOR YOUR SCHOOL AS IT WOULD LOOK IN THE YELLOW PAGES OF THIS PHONE BOOK.

WRITE A BOOKLET OF TIPS THAT WILL HELP PEOPLE USE THE TELEPHONE WISELY AND QUICKLY IN EMERGENCIES.

MAKE A *Guide to Telephone Etiquette.*

CHOOSE ONE NAME FROM THE PHONE BOOK. WRITE A DESCRIPTION OF THAT PERSON'S APPEARANCE, PERSONALITY AND LIFE.

CHOOSE TWO NAMES FROM THIS PHONE BOOK. WRITE A STORY ABOUT A ROMANCE BETWEEN THEM. TELL HOW THE TELEPHONE HELPED TO START THE ROMANCE.

PICK A RESTAURANT FROM THE YELLOW PAGES. WRITE AN ADVERTISEMENT FOR IT.

WRITE THE LYRICS FOR A SONG ABOUT TELEPHONE CALLS.

MAKE UP THREE 'DEAR OPERATOR' JOKES. WRITE THEM DOWN, THEN SHARE THEM WITH A FRIEND.

CHOOSE TWO NAMES FROM THE PHONE BOOK. WRITE A CONVERSATION THAT THE TWO MIGHT HAVE ON THE TELEPHONE.

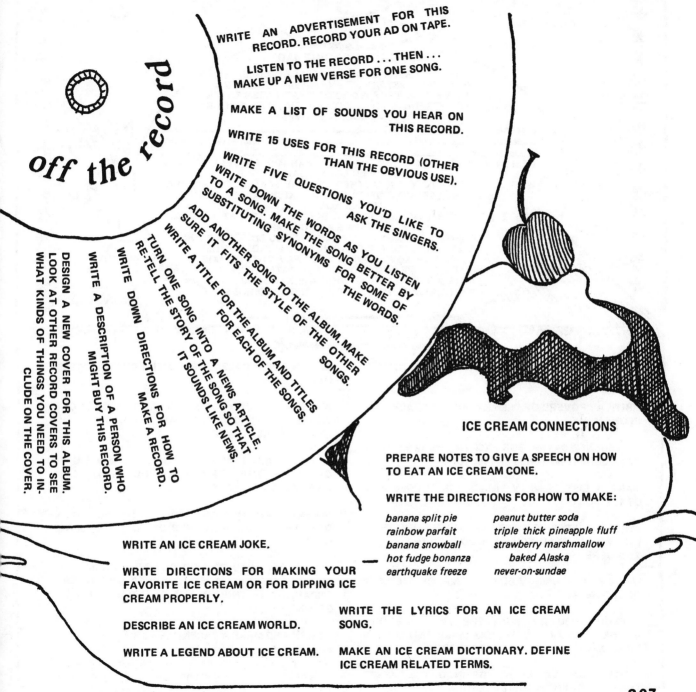

off the record

WRITE AN ADVERTISEMENT FOR THIS RECORD. RECORD YOUR AD ON TAPE.

LISTEN TO THE RECORD . . . THEN . . . MAKE UP A NEW VERSE FOR ONE SONG.

MAKE A LIST OF SOUNDS YOU HEAR ON THIS RECORD.

WRITE 15 USES FOR THIS RECORD (OTHER THAN THE OBVIOUS USE).

WRITE FIVE QUESTIONS YOU'D LIKE TO ASK THE SINGERS.

WRITE DOWN THE WORDS AS YOU LISTEN TO A SONG. MAKE THE SONG BETTER BY SUBSTITUTING SYNONYMS FOR SOME OF THE WORDS.

ADD ANOTHER SONG TO THE ALBUM. MAKE SURE IT FITS THE STYLE OF THE OTHER SONGS.

WRITE A TITLE FOR THE ALBUM AND TITLES FOR EACH OF THE SONGS.

TURN ONE SONG INTO A NEWS ARTICLE. RE-TELL THE STORY OF THE SONG SO THAT IT SOUNDS LIKE NEWS.

WRITE DOWN DIRECTIONS FOR HOW TO MAKE A RECORD.

WRITE A DESCRIPTION OF A PERSON WHO MIGHT BUY THIS RECORD.

DESIGN A NEW COVER FOR THIS ALBUM. LOOK AT OTHER RECORD COVERS TO SEE WHAT KINDS OF THINGS YOU NEED TO INCLUDE ON THE COVER.

ICE CREAM CONNECTIONS

PREPARE NOTES TO GIVE A SPEECH ON HOW TO EAT AN ICE CREAM CONE.

WRITE THE DIRECTIONS FOR HOW TO MAKE:

banana split pie	peanut butter soda
rainbow parfait	triple thick pineapple fluff
banana snowball	strawberry marshmallow
hot fudge bonanza	baked Alaska
earthquake freeze	never-on-sundae

WRITE AN ICE CREAM JOKE.

WRITE DIRECTIONS FOR MAKING YOUR FAVORITE ICE CREAM OR FOR DIPPING ICE CREAM PROPERLY.

DESCRIBE AN ICE CREAM WORLD.

WRITE A LEGEND ABOUT ICE CREAM.

WRITE THE LYRICS FOR AN ICE CREAM SONG.

MAKE AN ICE CREAM DICTIONARY. DEFINE ICE CREAM RELATED TERMS.

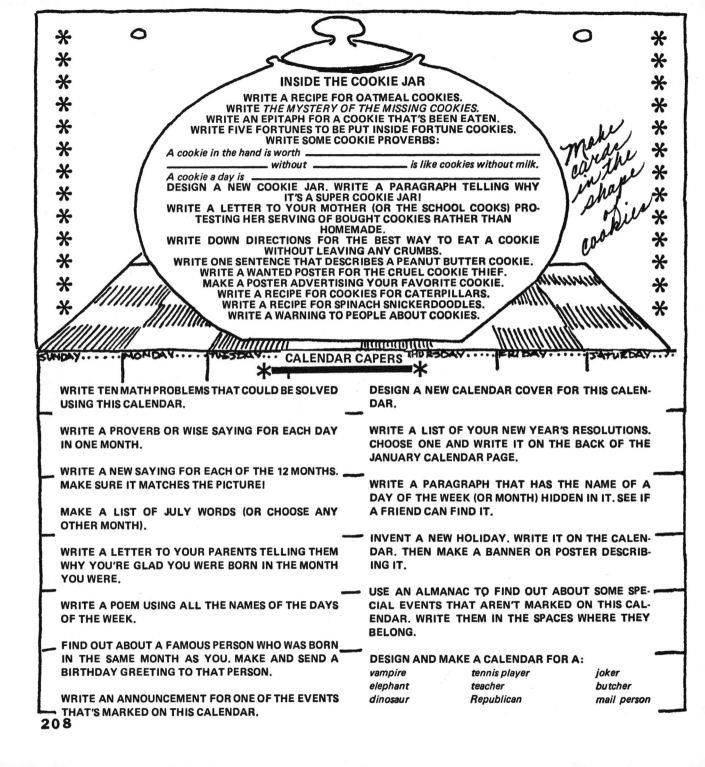

INSIDE THE COOKIE JAR

WRITE A RECIPE FOR OATMEAL COOKIES.
WRITE *THE MYSTERY OF THE MISSING COOKIES*.
WRITE AN EPITAPH FOR A COOKIE THAT'S BEEN EATEN.
WRITE FIVE FORTUNES TO BE PUT INSIDE FORTUNE COOKIES.
WRITE SOME COOKIE PROVERBS:

A cookie in the hand is worth _____
_____ without _____ is like cookies without milk.
A cookie a day is _____

DESIGN A NEW COOKIE JAR. WRITE A PARAGRAPH TELLING WHY
IT'S A SUPER COOKIE JAR!
WRITE A LETTER TO YOUR MOTHER (OR THE SCHOOL COOKS) PRO-
TESTING HER SERVING OF BOUGHT COOKIES RATHER THAN
HOMEMADE.
WRITE DOWN DIRECTIONS FOR THE BEST WAY TO EAT A COOKIE
WITHOUT LEAVING ANY CRUMBS.
WRITE ONE SENTENCE THAT DESCRIBES A PEANUT BUTTER COOKIE.
WRITE A WANTED POSTER FOR THE CRUEL COOKIE THIEF.
MAKE A POSTER ADVERTISING YOUR FAVORITE COOKIE.
WRITE A RECIPE FOR COOKIES FOR CATERPILLARS.
WRITE A RECIPE FOR SPINACH SNICKERDOODLES.
WRITE A WARNING TO PEOPLE ABOUT COOKIES.

Make cards in the shape of cookies

SUNDAY . . . . MONDAY . . . . TUESDAY . . . . **CALENDAR CAPERS** THURSDAY . . . . FRIDAY . . . . SATURDAY . . . .

WRITE TEN MATH PROBLEMS THAT COULD BE SOLVED USING THIS CALENDAR.

WRITE A PROVERB OR WISE SAYING FOR EACH DAY IN ONE MONTH.

WRITE A NEW SAYING FOR EACH OF THE 12 MONTHS. MAKE SURE IT MATCHES THE PICTURE!

MAKE A LIST OF JULY WORDS (OR CHOOSE ANY OTHER MONTH).

WRITE A LETTER TO YOUR PARENTS TELLING THEM WHY YOU'RE GLAD YOU WERE BORN IN THE MONTH YOU WERE.

WRITE A POEM USING ALL THE NAMES OF THE DAYS OF THE WEEK.

FIND OUT ABOUT A FAMOUS PERSON WHO WAS BORN IN THE SAME MONTH AS YOU. MAKE AND SEND A BIRTHDAY GREETING TO THAT PERSON.

WRITE AN ANNOUNCEMENT FOR ONE OF THE EVENTS THAT'S MARKED ON THIS CALENDAR.

DESIGN A NEW CALENDAR COVER FOR THIS CALEN-DAR.

WRITE A LIST OF YOUR NEW YEAR'S RESOLUTIONS. CHOOSE ONE AND WRITE IT ON THE BACK OF THE JANUARY CALENDAR PAGE.

WRITE A PARAGRAPH THAT HAS THE NAME OF A DAY OF THE WEEK (OR MONTH) HIDDEN IN IT. SEE IF A FRIEND CAN FIND IT.

INVENT A NEW HOLIDAY. WRITE IT ON THE CALEN-DAR. THEN MAKE A BANNER OR POSTER DESCRIB-ING IT.

USE AN ALMANAC TO FIND OUT ABOUT SOME SPE-CIAL EVENTS THAT AREN'T MARKED ON THIS CAL-ENDAR. WRITE THEM IN THE SPACES WHERE THEY BELONG.

DESIGN AND MAKE A CALENDAR FOR A:

vampire *tennis player* *joker*
elephant *teacher* *butcher*
dinosaur *Republican* *mail person*

hop a story...

went to see the mayor	this grumpy teacher	was carried off by pirates
said, "Never again!"	A fat, red lobster	got in a pillow fight
ate 59 fish sand-wiches	got locked in a closet with a pickle	on a picnic with a gorilla
saw a terrible giant	just barely escaped	floated away to Austria

Write story parts on an old shower curtain — place it on the floor and Hop a Story!

write on an old "Ace" bandage

BRAIN STRETCHERS

TELL SIX WAYS TO IMPROVE A SNOW SHOVEL.

EXPLAIN CHOCOLATE TO SOMEONE WHO'S NEVER SEEN OR TASTED IT.

WRITE A DEFINITION FOR "GARBILIOUS."

EXPLAIN HOW A TOENAIL COULD CATCH ON FIRE.

LIST 25 USES FOR A BRICK.

WRITE A LETTER TO A BARNACLE.

TELL HOW YOUR MIND IS LIKE AN ONION.

WRITE A POEM THAT TELLS HOW SUNSHINE SOUNDS.

WRITE A DINNER INVITATION FROM A MOUSE TO A CAT.

EXPLAIN WHY AN EARLOBE IS MORE VALUABLE THAN AN ELBOW.

Don't quit reading ....

The best part is yet to come! Actually, it's been happening all along. But we've been involved in some heavy idea-gathering and some time-consuming skill-building, and you may not have had a chance to take in the mountain top view because you're still sweating from the climb!

Stand still with me a moment, and enjoy the rewards of your work. Step back from the activity so you can watch just what it is that happens when you commit such energy to fertilizing communication skills.

Behold how kids grow! They collect ideas with increasing enthusiasm, turn their impressions into words more easily, share their writing more freely and express more openly. And isn't it a joy to glimpse those times when they go beyond you— when their expectations surpass yours or they choose to gamble on their own ideas rather than rest safely on yours, or they venture into projects without provocation? You hear less of, "I can't think of anything," and more of, "I'm not finished yet!"

And if you'll focus closely, I think you'll notice that they're not just learning to write—they're learning to live! For the processes of organizing and directing thinking for writing sharpen mental organizational skills needed for effectiveness in other areas of life. Those steps of collecting and sorting and censoring and evaluating are the same ones I use when I attempt to settle a disagreement between co-workers or when I decide my position on a political issue or prepare an agenda for a meeting with a publisher. It's the very same process that's going on when I formulate (and rehearse) an apology (or attack) to make to my husband after an argument, when I set arrangements for a trip, get a speech together for a workshop, gather my thoughts to make an important phone call or plan a dinner for twenty people.

Now look at your own growth! A special bonus of this whole writing process is what happens to the teacher's creativity and skill. I truly believe that you grow more than the kids! Your interest and your own effectiveness in written communication increase and you find yourself seeing possibilities in places you'd never thought to look. You change experiences into writing parties much more spontaneously and skillfully. Suddenly you're aware that your mouth knows what to ask and how to suggest and when to be silent.

211

As with any venture into new territory—especially those territories of human values, emotions and expressions, you're taking risks. You're trying things of which you're uncertain, toying with motivators that will yield new inventions, baring some parts of your own self as you grow and write with the kids. Every time you start a new writing journey you're launching into uncharted waters, even if you've used the idea before—because a new group of kids, a new time of the day, and a new moment make it unlike any other experience. You can expect uncertainty from the students too. There's apprehension any time someone creates a brand new thing. When they invent, and share themselves, they're risking disapproval, misunderstanding, disrespect—just as you risk lack of response to your idea, headshaking by the principal, disbelief of parents or icy stares from the teacher next door.

I encourage you to take the chances—and delight in them! For without them you miss the rewards. Don't be afraid to keep inching out further on the limb. If it starts to crack you can retreat in search of a stronger one. But if you stay on the ground you'll never see how the world looks from the top of the tree! Hold your breath, take the leap and enjoy the surprise of the outcome!

The risks will seem smaller; the going will be more comfortable, if you will:

REMEMBER THAT IT TAKES TIME. Alice Bergstrom, Amy Glazier and Erma Meisenheimer, three of my high school English teachers, gave hours to the cultivation of my written expression. They sat with me dozens of times, revising drafts, praising, suggesting. I believe that their dedication and patience were key factors in the development of the literary appreciation, persistence and self-discipline upon which I've called many many times since high school. But here I am, fifteen years later, still refining my writing skills! If, at the end of a school year, you're inclined to tear out your hair (or the kids') over still-rampant run-on sentences or sloppy spelling—DON'T! You can't expect mastery from a second, sixth, or even twelfth grader. Please don't berate yourself or the kids for the mistakes that keep recurring. LEARNING TO WRITE IS A LIFE-LONG PROCESS. Sometimes we teachers forget that our year with a child is just one small piece of that process.

TRUST THE KIDS. Your faith in the child is a key ingredient in her writing success and growth. BELIEVE that your students do have good ideas, that their lives do contain plenty of experiences worth writing, that they can express those experiences. BELIEVE that when you give them plenty of access to creative sources, many opportunities to write and refine, and consistent exposure to examples of effective communication, they will internalize the standards! You may not see it happening— the teacher next year or in five years may smell the flowers from the seeds you've planted. But they WILL grow! I have yet to meet a child who could dwell a year in a healthy, challenging writing climate without progressing in some way.

TRUST YOURSELF. BELIEVE that you can guide kids to better writing. Relax and have faith in your ability to ask the right questions, propose appropriate assignments, confront problems with wisdom. Ten years ago when Laura Keppner came to me with her paper and said, "Mrs. Frank, I can't think of anything else," I looked over her shoulder and—to be honest—couldn't think of anything either. So I put my arm around her shoulder and said, "Now Laura, if you'll go back to your seat and think real hard for three minutes, I'm sure you'll think of something."

Five years later, when Kenny Fiacco raised his hand with the same complaint, my mind erupted suggestions so fluently that he finally covered his ears and said, "Okay, okay, that's enough!" And just a year or two ago, I became conscious of what had happened—I was not nearly so afraid any more of kids' questions or hesitations. Gradually my skill and confidence had grown—because I'd talked to kids and eavesdropped on other teachers, and scrounged ideas, and tried some crazy things, and suffered through some terrible flops and tried again. And I've met scores of teachers who've shared a similar growth. I don't believe we're unique. I believe it happens to you and anyone else who dedicates time and care to writing with young people.

GIVE FREELY OF YOUR LOVE. Every child working toward personal expression should enjoy the company of at least one grown-up who delights in hearing words bump into one another and who's willing to share his or her enthusiasm for life and discovery. I was fortunate enough to have a mother and a few other such adults in my childhood (and post childhood). We can't count on that being the case for every child. You may be that one adult for many of your students. Don't let any one pass through your life or classroom without being touched by the special power of written words. And as you give them this, you'll receive from them in turn. I hope you'll let yourself be open to watch and laugh and cry and wonder at kids as they unfold their selves to you, to each other, to life.

With my applause for your writing ventures, my hopes for your successes, and my empathies for your mistakes—

Marge Frank

one more
very good idea

TIME CAPSULE

Today's date is _____

Presently, my life is _____

What I most like to do is _____

I value _____

These people are important to me _____

_____

I get angry about _____

My greatest joy these days is _____

Lately, I've hurt about _____

My best memory is _____

I worry about _____

Ten years from now, I hope to be _____

Before I die, I hope _____

Recently I've learned _____

Something else special about me right now is _____

_____

Not long ago, I was given an unexpected look at the Marge Frank of the past. My mom died suddenly, and as my father had been gone for years, we four children had to set about the task of sorting through and disposing of sixty-five years' worth of our parents' belongings. As we sat on the basement floor sniffling over diaries, laughing at old photographs and crying through love letters, I came upon a personal time capsule—a package Mother had saved and labeled, "Marjorie's Writings." I read through poems, essays and stories I hardly remembered writing, and became acquainted with the thoughts and fears and beliefs of a teenager who was myself. It provided me a priceless hour of learning more about who I am and how I came to be the person that is Marge Frank today.

Creating PERSONAL TIME CAPSULES is one of the nicest writing experiences you can offer yourself and your students. I recommend it for all ages of kids and grown-ups. Fill a box or envelope with some chosen piece of writing, a photograph or other treasured items and some statements that allow a person to record himself or herself as he is today. (See examples.) Then secure the package with sealing wax, label: DO NOT OPEN UNTIL _____, and send it home to be stashed away for twenty years.

IDEA INDEX